THE BODLEIAN DINNSHENCHALS

BY

WHITLEY STOKES

THE BODLEIAN DINNSHENCHAS.

THE Dinnshenchas is a collection of legends, in Middle-Irish prose and verse, about the names of noteworthy places in Ireland—plains, mountains, ridges, cairns, lakes, rivers, rapids, fords, estuaries, islands, and so forth. And the Bodleian Dinnshenchas is an unfinished copy of this collection preserved in the Bodleian library, in ff. 11-15 of the manuscript marked Rawlinson B. 506. This codex, once the property of Sir James Ware, is on parchment, and may have been written at the end of the fourteenth or the beginning of the fifteenth century. It contains, so far as one can judge by comparison with other copies, about one-third of the prose part of the work.

Five other copies of the Dinnshenchas are known, viz. :

LL., the copy in the Lebar Laignech, or the Book of Leinster, a MS. of the middle of the twelfth century, of which a facsimile, in which many of the leaves are misplaced, has been published by the Royal Irish Academy. Here most of the tales are told both in prose and in verse. But the prose versions, as found in the facsimile, are scattered through pp. 159, 160, and 165-170, and the so-called poems are in pp. 151-158, 161-164, and 191-216 ;

BB., the copy in the Book of Ballymote (a vellum of the end of the fourteenth century, in the library of the Royal Irish Academy), pp. 349-410 of the facsimile ;

H., H. 3. 3, a double-columned vellum in quarto, ff. 36, of (I should say) the beginning of the fifteenth century. For a loan of this copy, which belongs to the library of Trinity College, Dublin, I am indebted to the Board of that College ;

The Bodleian Dinnshenchas.

Lec., the copy in the Book of Lecan, a fifteenth-century vellum in the library of the Royal Irish Academy, pp. 461-525 ; and

R., the copy in the Irish MS. in the town library of Rennes, ff. 90-125. This excellent copy is perhaps fifty years older than BB. It has, unfortunately, lost a leaf between fo. 114 and fo. 115.[1] In R., as in BB., H., and Lec., prose and poems are placed together.

As to the date of the Dinnshenchas, O'Curry, *Lectures*, p. 108, states that it "was compiled at Tara about the year 550". But this is one of his ludicrous exaggerations. The reference s. v. *Laigin*, to the "King of Denmark and the Isles of the Foreigners", *i.e.*, the Hebrides, points to a period after the year 795. Dr. Petrie, *Tara Hill*, p. 105, advised in the matter by the cool-headed O'Donovan, calls the collection "a compilation of the 12th century"; and philological considerations prove that this is right, though some of the metrical materials may possibly be older. But whatever be their date, the documents as they stand are a storehouse of ancient Irish folk-lore, absolutely unaffected, so far as I can judge, by any foreign influence. See, for instance, in the following fragment, Nos. 1, 6, 7, 9, 10, 14, 15, 18, 22, 23, 24, 33, 36, 38, 43, 44, and 46. Hence, though the Bodleian Dinnshenchas contains only about a third of the prose part of the work, and though much of this third is silly or obscure, a faithful edition of the text, with a literal translation, will perhaps be acceptable to the readers of this Review.

[1] It is said by O'Reilly, in his *Irish Writers*, p. cxxiii, that there is a copy of the Dinnshenchas in the so-called Book of Hy-Maini, one of the Stowe MSS. now in the library of the Royal Irish Academy ; and Dr. Petrie, *Tara Hill*, p. 109, note 1, states that there is another copy in H. 2. 15, a MS. in the library of Trinity College, Dublin. But this copy is not mentioned in the description of H. 2. 15 given by O'Curry in his *Lectures*, p. 193, and I could not find it when I examined the latter MS. in last July. Lastly, M. Henri Gaidoz (*Revue Celtique*, vi, 113) says that there are two fragments of the Dinnshenchas in the Advocates' library, Edinburgh.

The Bodleian Dinnshenchas.

THE BODLEIAN DINNSHENCHAS.

(Rawl. B. 506, ff. 11ᵃ 1—15ᵃ 2.)

IN nomine[1] Patris *et* Filii *et* Spiritus Sancti amen sosis. SENCAS DINN ERINN DORIgni Aimirgin mac Amal[ga]dha, fili dona Deissib .1. fili Diarmata m*ei*c Cerbaill. Is e dorat algais f*or* Fintan m*a*c Bocra hi Tem*air* dia mbae mordail fer nErinn hi Tem*air* im Diarmait m*a*c Cerbaill ⁊ im Flann Febla m*a*c Scann-lain comarpa Pat*r*aic ⁊ im Cennfaelad m*a*c Ailella m*ei*c Eog*ain* m*ei*c Neill ⁊ im Finntan m*a*c Bochrai amm ardsenoir Er*enn,* ⁊ coro throsc teora laithi ⁊ teora aithche f*or* Finntan hi fiadhnaisi fer nErenn sceo m*a*cu ⁊ ingena hi Tem*air,* co ndeics*ed* do senchasa fira dind insi hErind, fodeig rola cach duine ⁊ cach dine di o aimsir Cessrai na hi*ngine* do G*r*ecaib Sceia—is i cetna rogab Er*inn* —co flath*ius* Diarmata m*ei*c Cerbaill. Unde poeta d*ix*it, Cuan .1. ua Lochan :

TEMAIR, TAILLTI, TIR n-oenaig.[2]

In the name of the Father, and the Son, and the Holy Ghost, amen, this below.

The story of the noteworthy steads of Ireland, which Amirgin MacAulay, a poet of the Dési, to wit, the poet of Diarmait, son of Cerball, composed.

He it is who made demand of Fintan, son of Bochra, at Tara, when there was a great gathering of the folk of Erin round Diarmait, son of Cerball, and Flann Febla, son of Scannlan, Saint Patrick's successor, and Cennfaelad, son of Ailill, son of Eogan, son of Níall, and Fintan, son of Bochra, the chief elder of Ireland. And Amirgin fasted on Fintan for three days and three nights in the presence of the men of Erin, both boys and girls, at Tara, so that Fintan might declare to him the true stories of the noteworthy steads of the Island of Erin, since he, Fintan, had dismissed (?) every person and every tribe from it from the time of Cessair, the maiden, of the Greeks of Scythia—sh̄ was the first that occupied Ireland—to the reign of Diarmait, son of Cerball. Hence said the poet, Cuan Ua Lochan,

"Tara, Teltown, land of the assembly," etc.

Also in BB. 349 a, and R. 90 a 1.

As to the Dési, see *Tofegr. Poems,* ed. O'Donovan, p. lxii, note 528.

Diarmait mac Cerbaill w.s king of Ireland from A.D. 5 $\sim$ to 553, and as Flann Febla, bishop of Armagh, died A.D. 704, they could not hav ben contemporaries.

As to Cennfaelad, see O'Curry's *Lectures,* pp. 47-4..

Fintan, son of Bochra, fabled to have survived the Deluge, and died in th seventh century after Christ.

Cessair, said to have been a granddaughter of Noah, and to have died A.M. 2242.

See O'Mahony's *Keating,* pp. 106, 107. Her connexion with the "Greeks of Scythia" is unexplained.

Cuan O'Lochain died A.D. 1024.

---

[1] MS. oimne.   [2] I omit twenty stanzas, chiefly composed on stupid strings of place-names, and having no relation to any existing copy of the Dinnshenchas.

The Bodleian Dinnshenchas.

[1. TEMUIR.]—TEAMUIR DIU .I. Muir Tea ingine Lugdach maic Itha dia luid la Geidi nOllgotha*ch*. Is 'na flaith sein ba bindidir la cach nduine i nErind guth araille beitis teta me*nn*chrota, ar mét in tsída ⁊ in tsamcuiri ⁊ in chaincomraic[1] ⁊ na cairdine robai do cach duine f*r*i aroile i nErind, ⁊ is airi[2] da*no* as [s]ruithiu cach mur .I. Tea-mur, [11ᵇ 1] ⁊ is uaisliu cach comarba a comarba, fobith[3] it e cétna[4] soerchuir doronta i nErind .I. cuir Tea ingine Lug*dach* ma*i*c Itha f*r*i Gede nOllgotha*ch*. Unde Tem*uir*.

Nó is Tea bean Erimoin ma*i*c Miledh Espa*in*e roadhn*acht* indte, et quod uerius est, ut poeta d*i*x*i*t :

> IN chetbean luid i n-uaigh[5] uair
> don cuan a Tur Breoga*in* bain,
> Tea Bregha, bean ind righ,
> dia[na]dh ainm Tem*uir* fir Fail.

TEMUIR, then, to wit, the *múr* 'rampart' of Tea, daughter of Lugaid, son of Ith, when she went with Geide the Loud-voiced. In his reign everyone in Erin deemed another's voice sweeter than strings of lutes would be, because of the greatness of the peace and quiet and the goodwill and friendship that each man had for the other in Ireland. Therefore, then, is Tea-múr more venerable than every rampart, and nobler than every heritor is its heritor, because the covenants of Tea, daughter of Lugaid, son of Ith, to Gede the Loud-voiced, were the first free covenants that were given in Erin.

Or Tea, wife of Erimon, son of Míl of Spain, was buried therein. This is truer, as the poet said :

> The first woman that went into a cold grave,
> Of the band from the Tower of white Breogan,
> Was Tea of Bregia, the wife of the King,
> From whom is the name ' true Temuir of Fál'.

Also in LL. 159 a.   The first paragraph is also in BB. 349 a, and in R. 90 a.
Temuir, gen. *Temrach*, now Tara, the palace of the monarchs of Ireland down to the reign of Diarmait, son of Fergus Cerrbél, when it was deserted owing to the curses of two saints, of whom one had been compelled by the king to surrender a murderer to justice. See the story of Diarmait's death, Egerton 1782, fo. 39 a, 2 ; O'Curry, *M. and C.*, ii, 237. As to Fál, Míl of Spain, Lugaid, Erimon, and Geide, see O'Mahony's *Keating*, pp. 81, 175, 183, 195, 197, 200, 204, 205, 233.

[2. MAG MBREG.]—Mag mBregh .I. Brega ainm daim Dile .I. Dil ingen Lugmannrach, dodechaidh a Tir Tairrngire, *nó* a tir Falga, la Tuilchaine druidh Conaire Moir ma*i*c Eitirsceoil ma*i*c Meissi Buachalla. I n-oenuair da*no* rogenir o mmath*air* in Dil sin ⁊ ruc in bo in loegh .I. Falga a ainm. Rocar iarum ingen ind rig in loeg sech na hindile olcena, ar rogenir a n-oenuair f*r*ia, ⁊

---

[1] MS. ambet ansida 7 insamcuirie 7 in caincomraith.   [2] MS. airie.
[3] MS. repeats.   [4] MS. cen*n*no.   [5] MS. uaidh.

*for*emidh Tulchaine a tabairt-si co t*r*cadh a dam le. Robo dual[1] do s*id*e in Morrigan, ꝗ rogaid-sium di tabairt do na himana sin co mbeith im-Maig Olgaide . 1. cetna ainm in maige,[2] (ꝗ rochar Brega in mag sin). Unde Mag mBregh dicitur.

No comad o Breoga m*ac* B*reogain* lasro slectad in mag no hainmnig[the]a, et quod uerius est, et unde poeta d*ix*t :

> Mag mBreog*a*, buaid ar mbunaidh,
> co Tuaim Tr*e*bain cen trelaim,
> sinds*er* na laech dar leru,
> Bre*o*ga, rogab *for* B*r*egaib.

*Mag mBr*e*g*, to wit, Brega, the name of Dil's ox, that is Dil, daughter of Lugh-mannair, who went from the Land of Promise, or from the land of Falga, with Tulchine, the druid of Conaire the Great, son of Etirscél, son of Mess Buachalla. In the same hour that Dil was born of her mother the cow brought forth the calf named Falga. So the king's daughter loved the calf beyond the rest of the cattle, for it was born at the same time (that she was) ; and Tulchine was unable to carry her off until he took the ox with her. The Morrígan was good unto him, and he prayed her to give him that drove so that it might be on Mag nOlgaidi, (which was) the first name of the plain; (and Brega loved that plain). Hence Mag mBreg is (so) called.

Or maybe it was named from Breogan, by whom the plain was cleared. This is truer, and hence the poet said :

> Mag Breoga, palm of our origin,
> As far as Tuaimm Trebain without weakness.[3]
> The eldest of the heroes over seas,
> Breoga, overcame Brega.

Also in BB. 406 b 45 ; Lec. 517 a ; R. 122 b 1.
Mag mBreg (also *Bregm* ꝗ), the name of a large plain in East Meath.
"The Land of Promise", one of the names for Fairy-land.
"The land of Falga" (or "of the men of Falga") seem to have been a name for the Isle of Man. O'Curry, *Lectures*, 588, note 172.
Conaire the Great, the hero of the Bruden Da-Derga, is said to have been king of Ireland, and killed by outlaws B.C. 40. His druid, or rather buffoon (*druth*), is described in LU. 92 b—93 a.
The Morrígan (*mori*, in, gl. lamia, Regina 215, fo. 1.), one of the Tuatha Dé Danann. See *infra*, s.v. Berba.
The Breogan here mentioned is, perhaps, the Span. Ea-corran in Keating, pp. 178, 179, 196.

[3. LAIGIN.]—Laigin a lag*i*nís uocatur . 1. d*o*naib laignib lethan-glassaib domb*er*tsat leo na Dubgaill dar muir anall . 1. da c*e*t ar *fichit cé*t a lín maroen la Labra*id* Loingsech M*oe*n, m*ac* Ailella Aine m*aic* Loega*iri* Luirc m*aic* Ug*aini* Moir. IS ond Labraidh sin ille fil gr*a*in ꝗ geretacht ꝗ omun ꝗ urfuath *for* Laig*nib* etir firu Er*enn*. Ar ba mor ind neim ꝗ in duabais ꝗ in duaig ro himredh

---

[1] dual . 1. maith, O'Dav. 79.
[2] MS. muigie.
[3] *trealamh*, weakness, O'R.

for Laig*nib*, *for*aib feisin ri tiachtu adocum nErind. Conid de asbeir ind rigfili Find mac Rossa Ru[a]idh :

Moen doen obanoed nimbodnos ardri orgg rigu rohud an loech huae luirc Labraidh lathi duabsi gasait inna lamaib laignai Laigein iarsin gniset catha cota ler lerga iath nErimoin is arlebur loicheit loingsech longais flaith Goedal [11ᵇ 2] gabais grib ind rig iath ancoil ua Luirc Labraid.

Loegairi Lorc, tra, meic [leg. mac] Ugaine Mair, is e senathair Laigen, unde Laigin d*icitur*.

No [i]s laigin ordai ⁊ airgididi doronsat cerdada Erinn do Labraid Loing*sech* dia tudcaid ⁊ Ernoll mac rig Danmarg ⁊ Indse Gall laiss. Et is e ro ort in rig*r*aid in nDind [Ríg], conid de na laigne sin ro imirthea *for* in rigraid i nDind Rig ⁊ *for* Cob*thach* Coelbreg rig Ere*nn* mac Uga*ini*, ⁊ conid o sain alle asbe*r*ar Laigi*n* f*r*iu, conidh de desin asbeir in sench*aid* :

> Labraidh Loi*ng*sec*h*, lor al-lin,
> ro ort Cob*thach* i nDind Righ,
> cosslu*ag* Laignech dar¹ linn Lir
> dib rohainmni[g]edh Laigi*n*.

> Tuaimm Tenma [a] aiṁ ria sin
> cnuic in² rog[n]iad inn orgain :
> is Dind Rig o sain alle
> ó marbadh³ na rigraidhe.

> Da cé*t* ar *fichit* cé*t* Gall
> co laig*nib* leathna⁴ leo anall :
> dona laignib tuctha insin
> de ata Laigi*n* *for* Laig*nib*.

Laigin, 'Leinster', so called from *laginae*, the broad green lances which the Black Foreigners brought with them over sea from the Continent. Two thousand and two hundred was their number along with Labraid Loingsech the Dumb, son of Ailill of Aine, son of Loegaire Lorc, son of Ugaine the Great. From the time of that Labraid, among (all) the men of Ireland, the Leinstermen are famed for championship and (for causing) horror, and fear, and dread. For great was the virulence and the ill-luck, and the misfortune that was inflicted upon the Leinstermen, on themselves, before Labraid came to Ireland. Wherefore saith the king-poet Find, son of Ross the Red, *Moen doen*, etc. [untranslatable by me].

Loegaire Lorc, then, son of Ugaine the Great, he is the ancestor of the Leinstermen. Hence 'Laigin' is so called.

Or it is the golden and silvern lances which the craftsmen of Erin made for Labraid Loingsech when he came along with Ernoll,

---

¹ MS. inserts in.   ² MS. ina.   ³ MS. ommarbadh.   ⁴ MS. repeats.

son of the King of Denmark and the Western Isles. And it is he that slew the king-folk in Dinn Ríg, and those lances were plied upon the king-folk in Dinn Ríg, and on Cobthach Slender-neck, King of Ireland, son of Ugaine. So thenceforward the Leinstermen are called Laigin. Wherefore saith the shanachie :

> Labraid Loingsech, sufficient their number,
> Slew Cobthach in Dinn Ríg,
> With a host of lancers over Ler's pool :
> From them Leinster was named.

> "Tuaimm Tenma" was the name before that
> Of the hill on which the slaughter was wrought.
> It is "Dinn Ríg" thenceforward,
> From the killing of the king-folk.

> Two thousand two hundred foreigners,
> With broad lances from the continent :
> From the lances which were borne there
> Hence the Leinstermen are called "Laigin".

Also in LL. 159 a ; BB. 357 a ; R. 94 b 2.
Laigin, now Leinster. *Insi Gall,* the Hebrides.
The first of the etymologies here given is adopted by Keating, p. 90.
As to Loegaire Lorc, Cobthach Slenderneck, and Labraid Loingsech, see Keating, pp. 250-254.
The remains of Dinn Rígh, " Height of Kings", one of the two royal seats in Leinster, are near Leighlin Bridge, to the west of the Barrow.
As to the slaughter which there took place, see LL. 48 b 10, 192 a 37, and 269 a.
" Ler's pool", a kenning for the sea.

[4. MAG LIPHI.]—Mag Lipi, cidh dia ta?
Ni *ansa* .1. LIPI i*ngen* Candain Curcaig[1] luid la Deltbanna m*ac* nDruchta, la dalem Conaire Moir riig Tem*ra*. A Sid Buidb er Femin dosaide. A[r] robo alaind leaa in mag dara tainic, ní[2] ro gaib *acht* a hainm fair.

> Lipi luchair, lor do blaid,
> i*ngen* Cannain cetcurc*aig :*
> dia hainm dogar[ar] a mag
> dia tudhcaid a tir Temrach.

"Mag Liphi," whence is (the name ?)
Not hard (to say).[3] Liphe, daughter of Cannan Curcach, eloped with Deltbanna, son of Drucht, with the cup-bearer of Conaire the Great, King of Tara. From Síd Buidb on Femen was he. Since the plain over which she passed seemed beautiful to her, she took nought save her name (to be) upon it.

---

[1] MS. curcaid.   [2] MS. nir.
[3] To save space, the translation of this common form will hence forward be omitted.

The Bodleian Dinnshenchas.

Liphe, the Bright, enough of fame,
Daughter of Cannan Cétchurcach.
From her name is called the plain
To which she came out of Tara's land.

Also in LL. 159 a 26; BB. 358 a 14; H. 17 b; and R. 95 a 1.
Mag Liphi, a plain in the co. Kildare, through which the river Liffey winds.
As to Conaire the Great, see above, No. 2.
Síd Buidb, "the Fairy mound of Bodb", one of the Tuath dé Danann; mentioned *infra*, Nos. 18, 20. *Femen*, a plain near Cashel, co. Tipperary.

[5. Loch Garman.]—Loch Carman, cid dia da?
Ni han*sa*. Garman m*a*c Bommallecce robaidedh ann la Cath*áir*
Mor ri Er*enn*, [uair rochoill in Garman] a rechtga ⁊ a dirgedetaid
imme oc Feiss Tem*rach* .1. mind oir na rigna tall a Tig Mid-
cuarta, ⁊ nomarbadh a mmuintir,[1] ar ba dib*er*gach ⁊ foglaid he.
Unde [poeta :]

> M*a*c Boma lecce luaidmi
> in ri Cath*air* romm-baidi,
> Garmman a ainm in ardfir
> tria baird*n*ib cona bad ri.[2]

No comma Carmman Glass m*a*c Degad on n-ainmni[g]der,
cuius frater Dea a quo Inbir nDea ⁊ Abann Dee hi crich Cualann.

Garman, son of Boimm Lecce, was drowned therein by Catháir
the Great, King of Ireland. For that Garman broke the king's
law and justice at the Feast of Tara, to wit, he stole the queen's
golden diadem out of Tech Midchuarta, and he used to kill her
household, for he was a brigand and a robber. Hence the poet :

> Boimm Lecce's son we announce :
> Catháir the king drowned him—
> Garman was the high man's name
> Thro' bardic poems—so that he might not be a king.

Or maybe it was named from Carman Glass, son of Dega, whose
brother was Dea, from whom (are named) Inber Dea and Abann
Dea, in the district of Cualu.

Also in LL. 159 a 37; BB. 370 b; Lec. 468 a; H. 24 b; and R. 102 b 1.
Loch Garman, now Wexford Haven, *Chron. Scot.*, p. 393.
Catháir the Great, over-king of Ireland, A.D. 122 (or 120).
Inber Dea, "estuary of the Dea", the mouth of the Vartry river, co. Wicklow.
Abhann Dea, the Vartry river.

[6. Fid nGaibli.]—Fidh nGaibli, cid dia ta?
Ni *ansa* .1. Gabol m*a*c Ethamdain m*a*ic Eciss tall g*r*inne
nAnge ingine in Dagdai rotheclainn s*íd*e do denam drochtai di,
ar in droctai[3] donidh in Dagda [12ᵃ 1] ni anad do tinsaitain cen
nobidh in muir *for* tuile, ni t[u]ctha banna ass cein ba haithbe

---

[1] MS. romarbad a mmuindtir.   [2] In the MS. this quatrain follows
the next sentence.   [3] Translated 'bridge' by Prof. Atkinson.

ann. Tarlaicc erchur iarum Gaible don grinni sin a Beluch Fu[a]laiscaig corragaib[1] foss, ⁊ co forbairt in chaill ass for cach leth ; conidh de sin ata Fidh nGaiblie innossa.

Noo, dono, ónd[2] abaind dianidh ainm Gobul fil i rind da cluana .1. Cluain Sasta ⁊ Cluana Moir, ⁊ tiruirthes tria Fidh nGaible, ut ipse Berchanus dixit :

> IS inmain in Gobul-sa,
> is uaidi [a] ainmnigud
> for leith ind feda-sa,[3]
> a rad ni ró :
> in gem-sa charmocail,
> i n-ucht na cluana-sa,
> tall[4] sluagh mor fó.

et quod est uerius.

Gabol, son of Ethamdan, son of Eces, stole the faggot which Ange, daughter of the Dagda, had gathered to make a tub there-out. For the tub which the Dagda had made would not cease from dripping while the sea was in flood, (though) not a drop came out of it during the ebb. Then Gaible made a cast of that faggot from Belach Fualascaig till it settled, and the wood grew out of it on every side. Hence Fid nGaibli is now (its name).

Or, then, from the river named Gobul, which is at the point of two *cluains* ('lawns'), to wit, Cluain Sasta and Cluain Mór. And it runs (?) through Fid nGaibli. As Berchán himself said :

> Dear is this Gobul :
> From it is the appellation
> On the half of this wood :
> To say so is not overmuch.
> This gem of carbuncle,
> In the breast of this lawn,
> Carried off a great, good host.

And this is truer.

Also in LL. 159 a 50 ; BB. 357 b 33 ; R. 95 a ; H. 17 a.

Fid nGaibli, anglicised Feeguile, the name of a wood in Leinster, in which S. Berchan erected the church of Clonsasta, situated in the parish of Cloonsast, barony of Coolestown and King's County. O'Don., *Topogr. Poems,* p. li ; *Book of Rights,* 214, note o.

The Dagda Mór, son of Ethliu (LL. 266b 38), was one of the leaders of the Tuatha Dé Danann. See *Revue Celtique,* xii, 125, and Keating, pp. 141, 143.

As to S. Berchán of Clonsast, see O'Curry, *Lectures,* pp. 353, 409, 412.

[7. MIDE.]—Mide, mac si[d]e Brata maic Deatha. Is air ba Midi a ainm, fodaig is e roata tenidh i n-Erind i tossach ria tascar clainde Nemid, co ro leath fo Erind uile, ⁊ co raba *secht* mbliadna for lassad, conidh on tenidh sin rohadnadh cach primteni [⁊] cach

---

[1] MS. corrabaib.   [2] MS. onda.   [3] MS. fiadasa.   [4] MS. talla.

p*r*imtellach i nErind, conid[d]esin dli[g]es a comarba [miach la
muic] cacha cleithi i nEr*inn*, co nderbratar druide Er*enn:* "Is
mide duin in tene-sa rofatad[1] isin tir." Luidh Mide ⁊ b*en*tais a
tengtha a cennaib na ndruadh, ⁊ dobeir leis co mbatar hi talmain
Uisnigh fo suide. Conid ann asbert Eriu ingen hUmoir, muime
Mide is*ed*e : "Is uais neach atat[h]ar sund [innocht]," ol sisi.
Unde Uis*n*ech ⁊ Mide dicuntur.

Mide, he was the son of Broth, son of Dëath. This is why
Mide was his name, because it is he that first lit a fire in Erin
before the expedition[2] of the children of Nemed. And the fire
spread throughout the whole of Erin, and for seven years was it
ablaze. And from that fire were kindled every chief fire and
every chief hearth in Ireland. Wherefore Mide's successor is
entitled to a sack (of corn) with a pig from every house-top in
Ireland. And the druids of Erin said: "Hateful (*mide*[3]) to us is
the fire that hath been kindled in the land." (Whereupon) Mide
went and cut the tongues out of the heads of the druids, and
took them with him, and buried them under him in the ground
of Uisnech. So then Mide's foster-mother, Eriu, daughter of
Umor, said this: "Haughty (*uais*) is someone (*nech*) to-night!"
saith she. Hence "Uisnech" and "Mide" are said.

Also in BB. 356 b ; H. 6 a ; and R. 94 a 2. In verse, LL. 199 b 34.
See O'Curry, *Manners and Customs*, ii, 191.
Mide, now Meath. *Uisnech*, now Usnagh Hill, co. West Meath.
The "children of Nemed", the second colonists of Ireland. See Keating, 121.
Eriu, daughter of Umor. She is called *Gairech* in R., *Gairi* in BB.

[8. EITHNE.]—Eith*n*e cidh diata?
Ni *ansa* .i. EITHNI, INGEN ECHACH Feidlig,[4] m*áthai*r Furb-
aidhi m*ai*c Concobai*r* ma*i*c Nessa, dochoidh o Emain Maiche
siar com-Meidb Cruach*an* dia hassait, fobith asb*er*t in drui f*r*ia
Clothraind m*ac* a seatha*r* dia marbad. Luidis da*no* dia fo-
thrucadh isin abaind, co tard in sruth buille fuirre, co ros-baidh.
Luidh do*no* Lu[g]aidh M*ac* con, co tucc in m*ac* trena toeb
*a*mmach .i. Furbuide, ⁊ is de sin ata Eith*n*e for[s]an abaind ⁊
Carnn Fur*baidi* uastu s*ed*e. Unde poeta d*ici*t :

Eith*n*e m*áthai*r ma*i*c in rig,
i*n*gen Echach Feidlig fir[5]:

---

[1] MS. indesa itened rofhata mide.

[2] *tascar* "expedition" : so the word is rendered in Ir. Nennius, p.
lxx, l. 16. O'Clery explains it as "a fleet", "an assembly", "emigrants".

[3] So O'Clery : *Midhe* .i. droichthene, "a bad fire", *Rev. Celt.*, v, 23.
But O'Curry, *Manners and Customs*, ii, 191, seems to render *mide* by
"insult". It is probably from an Old-Celtic *mitio-s*, cognate with Gr.
μῖσος from *mitsos*, and N.H.G. *meiden*.

[4] MS. EATHAC feidlid.   [5] MS. eath*ach* feidlid fir.

treithi tallad, borb in maid,
Furbuide mac Concobair.

Eithne, daughter of Eochaid Feidlech, mother of Furbaide, son of Conor mac Nessa, went from Emain Macha westward to Maive of Cruachu, for her lying-in, because the druid had said to Clothru that her sister's son would slay her. Then Eithne went to bathe in the river, whereupon the stream struck her and drowned her. Then Lugaid Mac con went and brought the boy, even Furbaide, forth through her side.[1] And hence "Eithne" is the name of the river, and "Furbaide's Cairn" over him. Hence said the poet :

> Eithne, the mother of the king's son,
> Daughter of true Eochaid Feidlech :
> Through her was cut away—savage the breach (?)—
> Furbaide, son of Conor.

This story is not, so far as I know, contained in any other copy of the Dinnshenchas.

The river Eithne, anglicised Inny, divides the present county of Longford from the western half of Westmeath, *Topogr. Poems*, p. ix.

Eochaid Feidlech, over-king of Ireland, had three daughters, Ethne, Clothru, and Medb. Ethne was married to Conor mac Nessa, by whom she had Furbaide, who afterwards, in vengeance for his father's death, slew his aunt Medb with a lump of *tanach* (hard cheese), LL. 124 b 34 ; O'Curry, *M. and C.*, ii, 240, 241, where O'Curry misrenders *tanach* by "stone".

As to Lugaid Mac-con, see the Battle of Magh Mucrama, *Rev. Celt.*, xiii. As to Furbaide's cairn on the top of Sliab Uillend, LL. 199 a 53.

⌊9. Bri Léith.⌋—Bri Leith, cid diata ?
Ni *ansa* .1. Liath mac Celtchair Cualand, mac flatha as coeme boe a sith nErind, rocarastar Bri Bruachbreac ing*in* [12ᵃ 2] Midir Morglondaig. Docoidh o ingenraid co mboi ic Fertai na nIngen h[i] toeb Temrach. Lotar na macoíme immach co Tulaich na hIarmaithrige, ⁊ nir' lecseat tableore sida Mideir secha sin, ar ba lir bechtheillinn il-lo² ainle [imfrecra] a ndibraicthe,³ co ro brissed ann Cachlan gilla Leith, [co n-apad. Imsói in ingen do Brí Leith, co ro bris a cride inti,] co ndebairt Liath : "Cenco roussa in ing*in*, is mo ai[n]m sea bias fuiri." Unde Brí Leith ⁊ Dind Cochlain.

> Liath mac Celt[ch]air Cualann coir
> carais *ingen* Midir móir.
> Bri Bruachbrecc, buadach co mblaidh,⁴
> nistas rainic mac Celt[ch]air.

Liath, son of Celtchar of Cualu, a prince's son, the fairest that dwelt in a fairy-mound in Erin, loved Brí Bruachbrec,

---

[1] The Cæsarean operation by which Furbaide was brought forth is mentioned in LL. 125a 3 (is triana táib tucsat na claidib in Furbaide) and 199a 45 (tuc a mmac tria taeb immach).

[2] MS. beichtheilliun ollo.   [3] MS. ndibergaigthe.   [4] MS. mblaigh.

daughter of Mider of the Mighty Deeds. She went from her maidens till she was at Fertae na n-Ingen ("The Maidens' Grave-mound") beside Tara. Liath and his boys went forth to Tulach na hIarmaithrige, and the slingers of Mider's fairy-mound did not let them pass, for as numerous as swarms (?) of bees on a beautiful day was the mutual answer of their castings. So Lochlán, Liath's gillie, was wounded by them, and he died. The maiden turns to Brí Léith, and there her heart broke. So Liath said : "Though I shall not attain the maiden, my name shall be upon her." Hence "Brí Léith" (Liath's Brí) and "Dinn Cochláin" (Cochlan's Height). .

> Liath, son of just Celtchar of Cualu,
> Loved great Mider's daughter,
> Brí Bruachbrecc, gifted, famous,
> Celtchar's son did not attain her.

Also in BB. 408 b 34 ; H. 68 b ; R. 124 b 1.

Brí Léith, west of Ardagh, in the present co. of Longford ; *Cualu* in the co. Wicklow. See O'Curry, *M. and C.*, iii, 350, 357, where he renders *bruachbrec* ("speckle-bellied") by " of the freckled face"; *Tulach na hIarmaithrige* by " Hill of Pursuit"; *tabieoiri* (derived from *taball*, " sling", W. *taſl*) by " warders", and *teillinn* (which he compares with W. *telyn*, "harp") by " humming wild bees".

As to the elf-king, Mider of Brí Léith, see Windisch's *Ir. Texte*, i, 115, 116, 876; and O'Curry, *M. and C.*, ii, 192-194 ; iii, 191. See also *infra*, s.v. *Mag Cruachan*.

[10. Tonn Clidna.]—Tonn Clidna, cid dia t[á]?

Ni *ansa* .1. Clidna ingen Genaind maíc Triuin dodechaidh a Tulaigh[1] da Roth, im-Maig Mell Tiri Tairrngiri la hIuchna Ciabfhaindech do rochtain Maíc ind Oc. Dorat sede breic immpe. R[os]hepain ceol di isind noidh credumai a mboi, conatuil fris ꝛ [im]roi a seol frithrosc co tudhchaidh timcell nErind fodes, co toracht Clidhna.

Is e tan connuargaib in murbrucht nemforcennach co ro scaile[2] fo cricha in betha frecnai[r]c. Fodeig roptar he tri mortuile Erind ind inbaid sin .1. Tuile Clidna ꝛ Tuili Ladhra[3] ꝛ Tuili Bale. *Acht* ní [i n-]aen uair conuargaibsit. Robed in tuile meodonach Tuile Ladra.

Dorimmart tra in tuile i n-ardda ꝛ fodaili fo tir nErind, co tarraid[4] in curach út ꝛ ind ingen ina collad ind, forsan tract, cor' baided ann sin Clidna Cruthach inge[n] Genainn.[5] Unde Tonn Clídna.

Clidna, daughter of Genann, son of Trén, went from Tulach dá Roth ("the Hill of Two Wheels") in the Pleasant Plain of the Land of Promise, with Iuchna Curly-locks, to reach Macc ind Oc. Iuchna practised guile upon her. He played music to

---

[1] MS. tulaidh.
[3] MS. Radhra.
[2] MS. nemforcennachneadact roscaile.
[4] MS. tarraig.
[5] MS. Gena ainn.

her in the boat of bronze wherein she lay, so that she slept. And he turned her course back, so that she went round Ireland southwards, till she came to Clidna. This was the time that the illimitable sea-burst arose and spread through the districts of the present world. Because there were at that season three great floods of Erin, to wit, Clidna's flood, and Ladra's flood, and Bale's flood. But not in the same hour did they arise. Ladra's flood was the middle one. So the flood pressed on aloft, and divided throughout the land of Erin, till it overtook yon boat with the girl asleep in it, on the strand, and there was drowned Clidna, the shapely daughter of Genann. Hence " Tonn Clidna" (Clidna's Wave).

Also in LL. 168 b 1 ; BB. 374 a 2 ; H. 27 b ; and R.

Tonn Chlidna, " the ancient name of a strand and the waves that broke over it, situated in or near the bay of *Cloch na Coillte* (Clonakilty), on the coast of the county of Cork" (O'Curry, *Lectures*, p. 306) ; " a loud surge in the bay of Glandore, much celebrated by the Irish poets" (O'Donovan, *Topogr. Poems*, p. lxvi ; Keating, pp. 205, 568). For the legend see *Four Masters*, A.D. 1557, note *h*, and *Magh Lena*, p. 95.

Iuchna. Another *Iuchna* seems an alias for Echaid Echbél (Horsemouth), as to whom see Cormac's *Glossary*, s.v. *fir*, and LL. 160 b 37, 169 b 46.

Macc ind Oc, sometimes called *in Mac Oc* or *Oengus Oc* (in LL. 266 a), son of the Dagda and Boann, *infra*, No. 36. Some of the many tales about him are noticed by Rhys, *Hibbert Lectures*, 144 *et seq.*

Ladra, the first man that died in Ireland, *Four Masters*, A.M. 2242.

Bale, formally = the Homeric Βαλιός, can hardly be the Bale mac Buain of a story printed in O'Curry's *Lectures*, pp. 472-74.

[11. SLIAB BLADMA.]—Sli*ab* Blad*ma* cid diata? Ni *ansa* .1. Bladma *nó* Blod m*a*c Con m*ai*c Caiss Clothmín[1] romarb buachaill Bregmael gabann Cuirchi m*ai*c Snithi rig Ua Fuatta. Doluid iarum ina noedin[2] corro gab h[i] Ross Bladma. Ross n-Air a ainm artus. Doluidh assen isin sliab. Unde est Sl*i*ab Blad*ma*.

Unde poeta dixit[3] :

Blod m*a*c Con m*ai*c Caiss Clothmin
romarb buach*ail* Bregmail bain,
gabann Cuirche moir m*ai*c Snithi,
rogab hi Ross Tiri inn air.

Nó is e Blodh m*a*c Breog*ain* is marb ann ꝛ is ua[d] ro hain-mniged[4] mons Bla*d*ma.

Bladma or Blod, son of Cú, son of Cass Clothmín, killed the cowherd of Bregmael, the smith of Cuirche. son of Snithe, King of Húi Fuatta. Then he went in his little boat till he set up at Ross Bladma—*Ross n-Áir*, " Wood of Slaughter," was its name at first. Thence he went to the mountain. Hence is " Sliab Bladma" (Bladma's Mountain).

---

[1] MS. clothaigmín. [2] MS. nodein. [3] MS. dr. [4] MS. hainmniag.

Whence the poet said :

> Blod, son of Cú, son of Cass Clothmín,
> Killed the cowherd of fair Bregmael,
> The smith of Cuirche Mór, son of Snithe :
> He set up at Ross Tíre ind Áir.[1]

Or it is Blod, son of Breogan, that died there ; and from him the mountain of Bladma was named.

Also in LL. 159 b 17 ; BB. 357 b 23 ; H. 17 a ; and R. 94 b 2.

Sliab Bladma, anglicised Slieve Bloom, in King's county, Keating, 457 ; " on the frontiers of the King's and Queen's Counties", O'Don. *Topogr. Poems,* lviii. Here rise the three rivers, Siuir, Nore, and Barrow.

Ross Tíre ind Air, "the Wood of the Land of the Slaughter". *Blodh mac Breogain,* spelt *Bladh* in Keating, p. 175

[12. Mag Raigni.]—Magh Raig*ni* cid dia ta ?

Ni *ansa* .i. Raigne romanach dodechaidh a[2] tirib Roman, ⁊ ruam ⁊ bacc f*r*i aiss, iar tuaslugadh in murgabail im[3] Thorinis nglain hi tirib F*r*anc, f*r*i t*r*i la. Adagastar opair n-aile samlaid do tabairt fair. Roteich iarum có toracht co hImlech ma*i*c Echonn. [12b 1] Robo druim fidhbaide uile essen, co *r*o selaigh Roigne he dia bacc ⁊ dia ramaind. Unde Mag Roigne.

> Esé roselaigh[4] in magh
> [Roigne] ro nirt, Romanach,
> dia luid a[5] Torinis tair
> *for* elud, *for* imgabail.

Raigne, the Roman, went from the lands of the Romans, with a spade and a billhook on his shoulder, after letting out, in three days, the inlet round Tours the Pure, in the lands of France. He feared that another work like it would be imposed upon him. So he fled till he came to Imliuch ma*i*c Echonn. That was (then) all a wooded ridge, so Roigne cut it down with his billhook and his spade. Hence " Mag Roigne" (Raigne's Plain).

> It is he who cleared the plain,
> Roigne the Mighty, the Roman,
> When he went eastward from Tours,
> Fleeing away, avoiding.

Also in LL. 159 b 28 ; BB. 373 a 25 ; H. 26 b ; Lec. 482 b ; and R. 104 a.

Magh Raigni is a plain in the barony of Kells, co. Kilkenny. See *Four Masters,* A.D. 859, note *t,* and the *Calendar of Oengus,* note at Sep. 17. *Imliuch maic Echonn,* not identified.

[13. Tethba.]—Tethbfa cídh dia ta ?

Ni *ansa.*[6] Teathfa ingen Ech*ach*[7] Aireaman[8] roscar mac

---

[1] "The Wood of the Land of the Slaughter."   [2] MS. dodech-aigh hi.   [3] MS. in.   [4] MS. ese*n* roselaidh.   [5] MS. hi.
[6] MS. repeats this and the five preceding words.   [7] MS. eath*ach.*
[8] marg. sup. *no* (?), Teathba *ingen* Ugaine.

Nectain Findgu[a]laig o Loch¹ Lein, Noisi a ainm. Roboi a muime *side* Eittech *ingen* Lennglaiss ma*ic* Luind, de Glomraide Tracta Tuirbi dó. Dochoidh la Tethfa ⁊ la Noissin ma*c* Ne*cht*ain Findgualaig,² co toracht Ard n-Umai. "Bid tesbaid do cumtuc[h] in tire-se mo dula-sa ass," ol ind ingen. "Ni ba fir son," ar a ceile, "ar ni teiseba do slonniud don tir. *Acht* bid teidmnech in dail³ brethri facbaisiu *for*sin tir sea." "Fot-lile cuma de,"⁴ *for* seat. Ba fir son disi, daigh atbath Etteach oc dul fodes .i. Ettech *ingen* Len[n]glaiss. Unde Tethba ⁊ Cenn Ettigh :

> Teathb[a] toga ban co mblaidh
> ingen Echa*ch*⁵ Airimain :
> hisin tir contoisi thair,
> ros-car Noissi ma*c* Ne*ch*tain.
> atbath Eittech i*ngen* Glaiss
> a Cind Etteig⁶ dia hingnais.

Tethba, daughter of Eochaid Airem, was loved by a son of Nechtán the White-shouldered, from Loch Léin, whose name was Nóisiu. His fostermother was Ettech, daughter of Lennglass, son of Lonn : of the Glomraide of Tracht Tuirbi was he. She went with Tethba and with Nóisiu, son of Nechtán the White-shouldered, till she came to Ard Umai.

"My going hence will be a loss to the beauty of this land," saith the girl.

"That will not be true," says her husband, "for thy name shall not be wanting to the land. But the worded doom which thou hast left on this land will be deadly."

"Grief for this will follow thee," say they.

That came true to her, for (her husband's fostermother) Ettech died when going southwards, even Ettech, daughter of Lennglass. Whence "Tethba" and "Cenn Etig".

> Tethba, choice of famous women,
> Daughter of Eochaid Aireman.
> In the land east he hearkens,
> Nóisiu, son of Nechtán, loved her.
> Ettech, daughter of Glass, died,
> At Cenn Ettig, of her absence.

Also in BB. 409 a 12 ; H. 68 b ; Lec. 521 a ; and R. 124 b 2.

Tethba, anglicised Teffa, a territory in the present counties of Westmeath and Longford ; O'Donovan, *Topogr. Poems,* p. ix. O'Curry, *Lectures*, 286, spells *Teabhtha*. *Loch Lein,* now the lake of Killarney, see *infra*, No. 18. *Tracht Tuirbi*, "Tuirbe's Strand", near Malahide.

Cenn Eitigh, now Kinnitty, in King's county. O'Curry, *Lectures,* p. 340; *Chron. Scot.*, p. 367.

Eochaid Airem, over-king of Ireland, A.M. 5070, according to the Four Masters.

¹ MS. lochoch.   ² MS. fingulai.   ³ MS. daeil.   ⁴ MS. ade.
⁵ MS. eath*ach*.   ⁶ MS. etteid.

The Bodleian Dinnshenchas.

NI ANSA .1.[1] Ainnind ⁊ Uar ⁊ Cimme Cethircenn, tri maic Umhor, do rigaib Fer m[B]olc. Do Greccaib al-lethcinel .1. Grecus[2] mac Point ⁊ Danaus[3] mac Point. IS e dano Danaus[3] sen Fer mBolc. Rogab ciniudh indala fir fortamlas ar aroile, con na ro leccsit in t-uisce sommblasta doib, fodaig is commus ⁊ is cacht bis hi tirib Grec for ind usci, ⁊ adachta fo doire .1. uir do taroidiud (sic!) for lecca loma co mbetis secht cubaid[4] in domni uire forraib.

Dodechatar iarum riasin cumachta moir sin dochum[5] nErind for eludh, ⁊ gnisit barcca doib dia mbolcaib, co tudhchatar co tirib Erenn ⁊ gabsat hic lochaib firuiscidib lochdoimnib lindglanib. Aindinn ic Loch Aindinn a Midi. Uar ic Loch Uair am-Miide ⁊ Cimmie la Connacta :

> Triar brathar, ba buan a ngloir,
> tri maic ardgasta Ugmoir,
> Ainninn, Uar am-Midhe annu,
> ocus Cimme a Conactu.

"Loch Anninn", whence is it?

Not hard (to say). Anninn and Uar, and Cimme Cethircenn, three sons of Umor, of the kings of the Fir Bolg. Of the Greeks was one of their two kindreds, to wit, Grecus, son of Pont, and Danaus, son of Pont. This Danaus was the ancestor of the Fir Bolg. The race of one of these two men prevailed over (that of the) other, so that they did not let them have the well-tasted water, because there is in the lands of the Greeks control and constraint over the water. And they were put under slavery, to wit, to drag mould (in leathern bags) on to bare flagstones, so that there should be seven cubits deep of mould upon them.

So they fled before that tyranny to Ireland, and they built them barques of their bags, and they came to the lands of Ireland and set up at loughs fresh-watered, profound, clear-pooled. Ainninn at Lough Ainninn, in Meath; Uar at Lough Uair, in Meath ; and Cimme, in Connaught.

> Three brothers, lasting their glory,
> Three high-brisk sons of Ugmor,
> Ainninn, Uar in Meath, to-day,
> And Cimme in Connaught.

Also in BB. 409 a 34 ; H. 69a ; Lec. 521 b ; and R. 125a 1.
As to the flight of the Fir Bolg, cf. Keating, p. 129.
Loch Ainninn, now Lough Ennell, in Westmeath. *Loch Uair*, now Lough Owel, in Westmeath. Turgeis (*Thórgils*) was drowned in it A.D. 847. *Loch Cimme*, now Lough Hackett, in the co. Galway.

---

[1] MS. repeats.   [2] MS. Grecas.   [3] MS. Tanais.   [4] MS. cumaid.
[5] MS. dodochum.

The Bodleian Dinnshenchas.

⌊15. BERBA.]—Berba, cidh dia ta ?
Ni *ansa* .1.[1] Berba his inti ro laitea na t*r*i nat*r*acha batar a
c*r*idi[b] Meich[i] m*aic* na Morigna, iarna bass do M*a*c Cecht im-
Maig Meichi. Mag Fertaigi da*no* ainm [12ᵇ 2] in maige sin pri*us*.
Delba[2] t*r*i cenn nat*r*ach batar for[s]na t*r*i cridib[3] batar im-Meichi,[4]
⅂ mina tairsedh a bas no oirbeordais na nath*racha* ina broind
*con*a facbadais anmanna beo i nErind. Coron loisc M*a*c Cecht
iarna marb*ad* i Maig Luadat,[5] ⅂ coro la a luaith lasin sruth út, co
rom-berb ⅂ coro dileag cach n-ainmidi[6] do anmandaib bai inti.
*Con*adh [de]sin ata Magh Lu[ad]at ⅂ Magh Méichi[7] ⅂ Berba.
Unde poeta d*ix*it :

> Cridi Meichi,[7] cruaidh in cned,
> isin Berba ro baided :
> a luaith iarna loscadh lib
> rocuir Mac Cecht cétguinigh.

Berba, into it were cast the three adders that abode in the
hearts of Méche, son of the Morrígain, after his death by Mac
Cecht in Mag Méchi (Mag Fertaigi, now was the name of that
plain formerly). The shapes of three adders' heads were on
the three hearts that were in Méche, and, unless his death had
occurred, the adders would have grown in his breast till they would
not have left an animal alive in Ireland. So after slaying him on
Mag Luadat, Mac Cecht burnt them (the hearts) and cast their
ashes with yon stream, and it boiled, and it dissolved every one of
the animals that were therein. Wherefore thence are "Mag
Luadat", and "Mag Méchi", and "Berba". Hence said the poet :

> Méche's hearts, hard the wound,
> Have been drowned in the Barrow ;
> Their ashes, after being burnt by you,
> Mac Cecht, slayer of a hundred, cast in.

Also in LL. 159 b 40 ; BB. 358 a ; H. 17 b ; and R. 95 a 2.
Berba, now the river Barrow. *Mag Luadat*, "probably the ancient name of the
plain now called Maghera cregan, situated near Newtown Stuart, in the barony of
Omagh and the co. of Tyrone." *Four Masters*, A.D. 1160, note *a*.
The *Morrígain*, v. *supra*, s.v. *Mag Breg*.
A *Mac Cecht*, one of the three kings of the Tuatha dé Danann, is slain by Airem.
Another Mac Cecht, King Conaire's champion, plays a great part in the *Bruden
da Derga*, LU. 89a, 97b, 98a.

⌊16. MAG FEMIN.]—Magh Fem*in*, cid dia da ? Ni ansa . 1.
FEMEN canas ro hainmnight[he]a ?
Ni *ansa* .1. Femen da*no* ⅂ Fera, da derbrathair . 1. da m*a*c
Moagaib m*aic* Dachair do claind Bratha m*aic* Deatha. Oen bacc
⅂ oen sluasat iairinn etur[r]u andis. In t*r*ath nobid Femean ic

---

[1] MS. repeats, putting *cid dia* for *cidh diata*.   [2] MS. Dlelb.
[3] MS. cri idib.   [4] MS. meithchi.   [5] MS. luagat,   [6] MS.
nanai*nn*midi,   [7] MS. Meithe,

fuilged nobidh Fera hic baccad.   In t*r*ath nobidh F*er*a ic baccad Femmen do*no* ic fuilg*ed*, ⁊ foceardad cectar de a mbacc ⁊ a sluasait inna himputh¹ techta dar in mag hir-Rae n-Urchuir dia-lailiu.   Unde [Mag] Femin ⁊ [Mag] Feara.

> Femen, Fera, fir fatha,
> do sil delbglan Deat[h]a,
> is eat doslectsat nammaig,
> Fera, Feme*n* a fidhbaidh.²

Mag Femin, whence is it?   Not hard.   Femen, whence was it named?   Not hard.   Femen, then, and Fera, two brothers, to wit, two sons of Moagab, son of Dachar of the clan of Brath, son of Dëath.   One billhook and one shovel of iron between the two. When Femen was shovelling, Fera was hacking.   When Fera was shovelling, Femen was hacking.   And each of them used to fling his billhook and his shovel in his proper turn to the other over the plain into Rae Urchuir ('Field of a cast').   Hence " Mag Femin", and " Mag Fera".

> Femen, Fera, truth of knowledge,
> Of the pure-formed seed of Dëath:
> It is they that cleared the two plains,
> Fera, Femen, of wood.

Also in LL. 168 b 28 ; BB. 373 b 7 ; H. 27 a ; Lec. 470 a ; and R. 104 a 2.
Magh Femin, that part of the present county of Tipperary which belongs to the diocese of Lismore.   *Topogr. Poems,* lxi.

[17. SLIAB MIS.]—Sliab Mís, cidh dia da ?
Ni *ansa* .i. .i. MIS INGEAN MAIREDHA, siur Each*ach*³ m*a*ic Maireda roan do eiss a himirge dia luid⁴ la Congancness m*a*c nDedad.⁵   IS *ed* da*no* forba ⁊ atharda fo*r*sa⁶ rir a fine ⁊ a aiccme, *for*sin sliab ut.   Unde Sliab Miss dicitur :

> Miandais Miss co mbruachaib [bla,]
> *in*gen morglicc Muireda,
> deis a himírce gan geiss
> lasin coemgein *C*ongancneiss.

Mis, daughter of Mairid, sister of Eochaid, son of Mairid, stayed with Congancness, son of Deda, after the flitting of her folk.   And the heritage and patrimony, for which she gave up her family and her kin, is on yon mountain.   Hence "Sliab Mis" is said.

> Mairid's very cunning daughter,
> Mis, with margins of land, remained (?)

---

¹ MS. himpuch.   ² MS. fidhbaigh.   ³ MS. eath*ach*.   ⁴ MS. olaid.
⁵ MS. ndeg*ad*.   ⁶ MS. forsra.

The Bodleian Dinnshenchas.

After her folk emigrated, without prohibition,
With the fair offspring Congancneiss.

Also in LL. 168 b 19; BB. 376 b 49; H. 30 a; Lec. 474 b; and R. 106 b 1.
Sliab Mis. Two mountains were so called, one in Antrim (now Slemish), the other between Tralee and Killarney, in Kerry. See O'Curry, *Lectures*, pp. 394, 448; Keating, p. 201; O'Donovan, *Four Masters*, A.M. 4319.
Eochaid, son of Mairid. See the tale of his death, LU. 39 a *et seq.*

[18. LOCH LEIN.]—Loch Lein, cidh dia da?
Ni *ansa* .1. LOCH .1. Lein Linnfiaccla[i]ch m*aic* Bain Bolgaig
m*aic* Bannaig, cerd sen Side Buidb. Is e romboi fo[1] loch ic
denam niamlesstair [Fainde] Foltlibre ingine Flidaise[2] [13a 1].
Iar scur a op*r*i cach n-aidhce [focheirded] a hindeoin uad [co
hIndeoin na nDeisi] cosin feirt, ⁊ na f*r*asa foeirded[3] iarsin din
muin it eat na nemanna rosilat ann di. Nithnemannach dorigni
a cetna oc slaidi cu[a]ich Concoba*i*r m*ai*c Nessa a [th]uaid. Is
do sin ata [Loch] Lein ⁊ Ind[eo]i*n* na nDeissi. Unde Loch Len.

Len Linfiacclach m*ac* Bain Bolcaig[4]
fo Loch Lein li*n*diacac (?) leir.
cerd cen ciargestul, cen cain,
fodail niamlesstair fo neim.

The Lake, that is, of Lén Linnfiaclach, son of Ban Bolgach,
son of Bannach. He was the craftsman of Síd Buidb ("Bodb's
Fairy-mound"). It is he that was under the lake making the
bright vessel of Fann the Long-haired, daughter of Flidais.
Every night, after quitting his work, he used to fling his anvil
away to the Indeoin na nDése ("The Anvil of the Dési"), to the
mound; and the showers which, thereafter, it used to cast forth
from the back, they are the pearls which were there sown by it.
Nithnemannach did the same in beating out the cup of Conor
mac Nessa in the north. Hence is "Loch Léin" and the "Anvil
of the Dési".

Lén Linnfiaclach, son of Ban Bolgach,
Under Lough Léin . . . manifest,
A craftsman without a black deed, without reproach,
Distributed bright vessels under heaven.

Also in BB. 379 a 5; H. 32 b; Lec. 477 a; and R. 108 a 1. Versified, LL. 154 b 35.
Loch Léin, now the Lake of Killarney. See O'Curry, *Lectures*, 75.
Síd Buidb, v. *supra*, No. 4.
Indéoin na nDése, now Mullach Inde óna (anglicised Mullaghnoney), near
Clonmel, co. Tipperary. *Four Masters*, A.D. 852; *Chron. Scot.*, p. 389. See
O'Curry, *M. and C.*, iii, 203. For *cerd sen side Buidb* H. has *cei d-side Buidb*.
The text seems corrupt. For *for loch* H. has *isin loch*. The third and fourth
sentences stand thus in H.:

---

[1] MS. for.   [2] MS. ingine foltlibri fligais.   [3] MS. foceiredid.
[4] MS. bolcaid.

IAR scur a oibre cach n-oidhche foceirded oad a inneoin sair co hIndeoin na nDesi, cusan fert, et tri frosa foceirdedh .i. fros uisci et fros teined 7 fros do nemoind chorcorglain. *Ocus* donit⌐h⌐ Nemannach an cetno ac sloide chuaích Concobair.

Every night, after quitting his work, he would fling his anvil from him eastwards, to Indeoin na nDése, to the mound. And three showers it used to cast off, to wit, a shower of water and a shower of fire and a shower of pure-purple pearl. And Nemannach used to do the same when beating (out) Conor's cup.

[19. SLIAB CUA.]—Sliab Cua, canas rohainmni[g]ed?
Ni *ansa* .1. Cua Cennmar m*a*c Broccalaig[1] Cringluinig, dalta Boibli m*aic* Birurchai. Tainic boar mor i nHerinn i n-aimsir *Con*gail Clairingnig, *con*a frith act oen tarb ⁊ oen samaisc i nGlend t-Samaisce.[2] Rofoeided g*ach* dalta a den*us* dia coimed. Intan doroact Cua Cennmar cuairt a commeta rofell f*or*aib. Ros-ruc leiss co ndernai[3] brothlaig f*or*aib,[4] ⁊ dos-fuaid isin tsleib. unde Sl*iab* C*ua*.

> Cua Cennmar co cruth cain,
> m*a*c Br[o]ccalaig Cringlunma[i]r,
> da[l]ta duaidh a boin 'sa tsleib :
> robo dalta co ndallceill.

Cua Great-head, son of Broccshalach Wither-kneed, fosterling of Boible, son of Birurchae. In the time of Conall the Flat-nailed, a great murrain invaded Ireland, so that there was found only one bull and one heifer in Glenn Samaisce. Each of Boible's fosterlings was sent in his turn to guard the cattle. When Cua Great-head came to his turn to guard them, he acted treacherously regarding them. He took them with him, and made a cooking-pit for them, and devoured them on the mountain. Whence "Sliab Cua".

> Cua Great-head, with a fair form,
> Son of Broccsalach Wither-kneed.
> A fosterling who devoured his cow on the mountain.
> He was a fosterling with a blind reason.

Also in LL. 169 a 1.
Sliab Cua, a mountain, now Slieve Gua, in the co. of Waterford.   *Glenn Samaisce*, hardly the valley so named, in Cualnge in Ulster.

[20. LUIMNECH.]—Luimnech, cid dia ta?
Ni *ansa* .1. LUIMNECH de asberar dia rofas in [i]mmarbaig *etar* na [dá] fhéinidd[5] robatar ic rígh[6] Mum*a*n ⁊ righ nOllnecmacht. Rind ⁊ Foeb[ur] a n-anmann, da derbrath*air* eat andis .1. da m*a*c Smucaille m*aic* Baccduib. Rogab indala n-oi amsai mBuidb a Sidh Femin a Mu[m]ain. Gabaiss alaile amhsaige hOcailli

---

[1] MS. brorcalaid. (the first *d* dotted).   [2] MS. tsamai aisca.   [3] MS. conder*n*naid
[4] MS. inserts isin tsleib.   [5] MS. feindig (*f* dotted).   [6] MS. hic*r*ich.

Connachtaib a Síd¹ Cruachan int[sa]inruth. Con tardsat a ceird muccada for aird con targlamsat dail móir imon cocrich andes ꝗ atuaith immun n-inbir, gac[h] laech co lumain i cechtar na da dal. Foruabratar cluiche imon sruth. His e sin tan tainic a thuile lais oc tindtud, conid and atbertatar na derccaide san chan im sruth na Sinda² de Tul Tuindi co n-athi buille: "Is luimnechda in t-inbiur!"

Nó intan batar na trenfhir ic imargail con tompacht tonn tuile a sciatha dib, co ndebratar in da rig don cnucc dianidh ainm Tul Tuinde: "Is luimnechda" .ɪ. i[s] sciathach "in t-inber indorsa," ol seat.

Isi sein danu in cocrich cert in da coiced, unde Luimnech dicitur.

> Dia da Luimnech, liss na long,
> isam cuimnech cen imroll ;
> dia sui in sruth, cen tiacra cnedh,
> sciatha mora na miled.

Luimnech, hence is it (so) called, when the contest arose between the two champions who were with the king of Munster and the king of Connaught. Rind and Foebur were their names; two brothers were the twain, to wit, two sons of Smucaill, son of Baccdub. One of the twain took service with Bodb of Síd Femin in Munster. The other took service with Ocaill in Connaught, of Síd Cruachan especially. So they displayed their swineherd's art, and collected, from south and from north, a great assembly at the frontier at the inver, every hero in each of the two assemblies having a shield (lumain). They began the game at the stream (of the Shannon). That was the time when the flood came at the turn (of the tide). So then said the onlookers, to and fro, from Tul Tuinne, by the stream of the Shannon, with its deadly blow: "The inver now is full of shields (luimnechda)!"

Or, when the champions were contending, a wave of the flood tore their shields away from them. So the two kings exclaimed from the hillock named Tul Tuinne ("Front of the Wave"): "The inver is now luimnechda," that is, "full of shields," say they.

That, then, is the right mering of the two provinces (Munster and Connaught). Hence "Luimnech" is said.

> Whence is 'Luimnech', the garth of the ships,
> I am mindful without error:
> When the stream turned, without affliction of wounds,
> The great shields of the soldiers.

Also in BB. 379 a; H. 33 a; Lec. 477 b; and R. 108 a 2. Versified, LL. 155 a 25. Bodb of Síd Femin, the fairy-king above mentioned, No. 4. Ocaill of Síd

---

¹ MS. sig.　　² The gen. sg. of a fem. u-stem=Skr. sindhu F. river.

Cruachan, another fairy-king. Both occur in the *Cophur in dá muccida*, ed. Windisch, *Irische Texte*, 3rd Series, part i, pp. 235 *et seq.*

Luimnech, anciently applied to the lower Shannon only. O'Donovan, *Topogr. Poems*, p. l.

According to the Book of Leinster, 247 a, the two champions passed through various existences, and were variously named. They were Rucht and Runce when they were two swineherds; Ingen and Eitte ("Talon and Wing") when they were two kites (hawks?); Bled and Blod when they were two beasts under seas; Rind and Faebur ("Point and Edge") when they were two champions; Scáth and Sciath ("Shadow and Shield") when they were two phantoms; Crunniuc and Tunniuc when they were two worms; and the Whitehorn of Ai and the Dun of Cualnge when they were the two bulls famed in the Táin Bó Cualnge.

[21. SLIAB NECHTGA.]—[13ᵃ 2] Sliab nEchtga can[as] rohainm-*niged ?*

Ni *ansa* .1. ECHTGA hUathach ingean Aurscathaigh[1] *maic* Tindi Truim do Tuath*ai*b Dea Donand. Is ann ro alt, hi Cúil[2] Echtair hi toeb Nenta, la Moach Moelchenn. Roboi deogbaire Gaind ⁊ Sengaind oca cuingid .1. Ferg*us* mac Ruide Lusca Beist. Is[3] arai asb*er*ti Lusca P[ei]st de fobith peist ro alt assa lusca .1. assa noedend*acht*, inna medhon.

Rofáim ind ingin feiss da*no* leissium fodaig feraind cuchchaire ⁊ deoghbaire boi ina laim o ri n-Olnecc*macht* .1. o Moen co fairrgi insin. Ni boi da*no* innmais laiss ⁊ boi ferann. Boi, da*no*, innmais lasind ingin ⁊ ni boi ferann na horba, ⁊ issed connaitecht fair .1. fother fossad cona febaib. Roherbad di assliab ut .1. Echtga, ⁊ b*er*tair di bai ann indorsa .1. bó anntuaith ⁊ bó annddess, ⁊ b*er*idh in bó atuaith *t*rian mblechta sech in mboin andess. Unde Sliab nEchta.

> Echtga Uathach os gach blaidh,
> ingen airdairc Urscathaig[4] ;
> si conaitecht sliab nach slait
> *for* Ferg*us* 'na turfochraic.

Echta the Awful, daughter of Aurscothach, son of Tinne Tromm of the Tuatha Dé Donann. She was reared at Cúil Echtair beside Nenta, by Moach Baldhead. The cupbearer of Gann and Sengann was wooing her, even Fergus son of Ruide, Lusca Béist. Why he was called "Lusca Béist" was because from his cradle (*lusca*), that is, from his infancy, he nourished a monster (*béist*) in his inside.

Now the girl consented to marry him for sake of the cook-and-cupbearer's land that he held from the King of Connaught. It extended from Moen to the sea. Fergus had no (movable) wealth, though he had land. The girl, however, had wealth, though she had neither land nor heritage. And this is what she demanded of him, even a firm *fother* (?) with its stock. Yon mountain, even Echtga, was entrusted to her, and two cows are now

---

¹ MS. Aurscathaidh.   ² MS. ciuil.   ³ MS. beisti.
⁴ MS. Urscathaid

The Bodleian Dinnshenchas.

brought there, a cow from the north and a cow from the south. And the cow from the north yields a third more milk than the cow from the south. Hence "Sliab Echtga".

> Echta the Awful, above every fame,
> Conspicuous daughter of Aurscathach,
> She demanded a mountain, which she robbed not,
> From Fergus, as her bride-price.

Also in LL. 167 a 43 ; BB. 381 b ; H. 40 a ; Lec. 480 b ; and R. 110 a 1. Sliab nEchtga, anglicised Slieve Aughty, the name of a mountainous district on the confines of Galway and Clare. O'Don., *Topogr. Poems*, xliv ; *Four Masters*, A.D. 1598, p. 2054, note *h*. The story of the two milch cows accounts for the rivername *Abhainn dá Loilgheach*, which divides the fertile from the barren part of Slieve Aughty.

[22. MAG NAIDNE.]—Mag nAidhne, canas rohainmni[g]ed ?
Ni *ansa* .1. Aidne mac Allgubai maic Eithriuil, is e cetfer noatad[1] tenidh ar tus dogres ria maccu Miled Espandai in gach baili i ngabdais longport, fobithin ni ba hecen dó acht a basa for araili dogrés, co teigtis crithri[2] tenidh tennalda a suilib a mér, commdar meide fiadubla adnui hi tus a mbuana, conid he sin slechtais in mag. Unde Mag nAidne dicitur. *No* comad 'ar n-ecc ann nohammni[g]thea, et quod est uerius.

> Mac Allguba, bai da brig,
> meic Eithriuil aib airdmin,
> cedna toisseach tricheim tenn
> reia macaib Miled mortenn.

Aidne, son of Allguba, son of Ethrél, he is the first man that kindled fire continually before the sons of Míl the Spaniard, in every stead wherein they pitched a camp. Because he needed only to put one of his palms over the other, whereupon sparks of fire, as from a firebrand, would come out of his knuckles,[3] and the sparks were as large as fresh wild apples at the beginning of their harvesting. And he it is that cleared the plain. Whence "Mag Aidne" (Aidne's Plain) is said. Or mayhap it was so named after his death thereon. This is truer.

> The son of Allguba, such was his virtue,
> Son of Ethrél beautiful, exceeding gentle,
> Was the first chief who lighted a blaze
> Before the sons of mighty Míl."

Also in BB. 382 b ; H. 41 a ; Lec. 482 b ; R. 110 b. Versified, LL. 156 b 37. *Mag nAidne*, "a level district in the present co. of Galway, all comprised in the diocese of Kilmacduagh." *Four Masters*, A.M. 3727, note *m*. *Ethrél*, perhaps the Eithrial said to have been over-king of Ireland, A.M. 3530.

[23. PORT LAIRGE.]—Port Lairge, canas rohainmni[g]ed ?
Ni *ansa* .1. Fectas doluid Roth mac Cithing, maic rig Insi

---

[1] MS. noataid.   [2] MS. crithni.   [3] Lit. eyes of his fingers.

VOL. III.   K K

Aine a tirib iath Fomorach la hairchind tiri do chu[a]ird a coic*r*iche, co cuala [inní] .1. dord na murduchunn do Muir n-Icht. Is *ed* in fuath atconnairc .1. in murduchund fo deilb ingine m*a*c[d]acta. Is blaithem [u]as li*n*d ɔ ichtar brotharluibnech bíastaide fothi¹ [13ᵇ 1] fo lind. Co n[d]uadar na biasda he, co ndaralsat he ina aigib, co ruige ın fairge a da lairg cosin port hut, ɔ no[t]hallad da[il] céd *for* mael gach cnama. Unde Port Lairge dicitur.

> IS de gongarthar in cuan
> Portt Lairge na leburtuagh,²
> ann frith laarg, lithaing lir,
> Ruith m*a*i*c* Cithaing cetguinig.

Once upon a time, Roth, son of Citheng, son of the King of Inis Aine, went from the lands of the Fomorian countries with a chief (?) of the land to go round his boundary, when he heard somewhat, the burden of the mermaids of the Ictian Sea. This is the form that he beheld, the mermaid with the shape of a grown-up girl. Above the water she was most smooth ; but below the water her lower parts were hairy-clawed and bestial. So the monsters devoured him and cast him away in joints. And the sea carried his two thigh-bones to yonder port, and the share of a hundred would fit on the flat³ of each bone. Hence Port Lairge ("Port of the Thighbone") is (so) called.

> Hence is the haven called
> Port Lairge of the broad axes.
> *There* was found a thigh, ... of the sea,
> Of Roth, son of Citheng the hundred-slayer.

Al o in LL. 169a 11. A variant in BB. 372 b; H. 26 a ; Lec. 470 a ; R. 103 b 2. *Por* *Lairge*, now Waterford. The "Ictian Sea", the Channel.
In R., etc., the mermaids are described as having yellow hair and white skins. and they ring a wonderful burden to Roth, so that he falls asleep.
The penultimate sentence is obscure. LL. has : nothallad dáil chét for mael cech cnama. BB. has : notallad ol .c. i maol a chnama. H. has : notall*a*dh oul cet a maol a cnamho. Lec. has : nothallad ol .c. a maelchnama. R. has : notalladh ol cet a mael a chnamha. Here *ol*, *oul*, *ol*, can only mean "drink".

[24. SEIG MOSSAD.]--Seig Mossadh canass r[o]hainmn*iged*?
Ni *ansa* .1. Mossad mac Main m*a*i*c* Fleiscci Findi fofhu[a]ir in seig im-Muigh Eoin. Rom-biath ɔ roforbairt co n-ith*ed* na groighi ɔ na tainte ɔ na daine deissib ɔ t*r*iaraib, ɔ o na fu[a]ir fodeoidh⁴ ní condeossadh conimsoi fria aite .1. Mossad .1. Mossad m*a*c Main isan maig. Unde Mag Mossadh ɔ Seig Moss*ad*.

> Mossad m*a*c Main, g*r*inne gel,
> m*a*c Fleiscci Findi, fo fer,

---

¹ MS. brotharluaimnech biassdaie foti.   ² MS. leburtuadh.
³ Perhaps the popliteal area.   ⁴ MS. fodeoigh.

The Bodleian Dinnshenchas.

alais seig fri[1] seilc subaigh,
robo mein rí mor-fub*aid*.

Mossad, son of Maen, son of Flesc Find ("White Rod") found the hawk on Mag Eoin. He fed it and nourished it till it used to eat the herds of horses, and the droves of cattle, and the human beings by twos and threes. And when at last it found nothing to devour, it turned on the plain against its fosterer Mossad, even Mossad, son of Maen. Hence *Mag Mossad* (" Mossad's Plain") and *Séig Mossad* (" Mossad's Hawk").

Mossad, son of Maen, a fair faggot,
Son of Flesc Find, a good man,
Nurtured a hawk for joyous hunting :
Its desire was in great destruction.

Also in LL. 160 b 37, and Lec. 523 b. LL. adds that the place may have been named from Mossad, a gillie of Eogan Taidlech.
I cannot identify Mag Eoin (= Fid Eoin, Lec.) or Mag Mossad.

[25. MAG MAIN.]—Mag Main, cidh dia ta ?
Ni *ansa* .i. Moen Morgnimach fer berrtha *nó* berrthoir mac Miledh, is e *cét*na fer no ber[r]ad i nEirind .i. iar tascur mac Miled. Is e da*no* cetfer rober*r*ad i nErind, Fobarr Foltcain. Is e da*no* cedluag be*r*rtha tuccad art*us* i nErind .i. Be*r*[r]amain .i. ferann i c*u*main a be*r*rtha. Marb da*no* im-Muig Moen cen brec.
Nó comad[2] il-log a be*r*rtha taithi in mag ac caillig ta*ntu*m, conid de sin ata Moenmag ˥ Be*r*ramain.
No comad il-logh a berrthorachta do Maen do be*r*tais Ma*i*c Miled Be*r*ramain do Moen. Et quod est uerius.

Ba marb Moen co mine ngal
for Mag Main atcu[a]lamar :
fo[fh]uair cen debtha[3] tre baig
il-log be*r*rtha[4] Ber[r]amain.

Maen of the Mighty-deeds, the barber of the sons of Míl : he was the first man who shaved (others) in Erin, to wit, after the expedition of the sons of Míl. Now the first man who was shaved in Ireland was Fobarr Foltchain. This is the first barber's fee that was given in Erin, to wit, Berramain, that is, a land in reward (*cumáin*) of his shaving (*berrtha*). He died, then, without a lie, in Mag Móin.
Or maybe it was recompense of his shaving that the plain . . . . . . only : whence are "Moenmag" and "Berramain".
Or maybe it was in wage for his barbering that the sons of Míl gave Berramain to Moen. And this is truer.

Moen was dead, with fineness of valours,
On Mag Moen (as) we have heard.

---

[1] MS. f*r*is.   [2] MS. coma ad.   [3] MS. deatba.   [4] MS. be*r*rta.

K K 2

He obtained without disputes through battle
Berramain as a reward for shaving.

Also in LL. 167 b 6 ; BB. 382 b 29 ; H. 41 b ; Lec. 483 a, where the place is
called *Moenmag*, now Moinmoy, a territory lying round Loughrea, in the co. of
Galway. *Berramain*, near Tralee ; see *Rev. Celtique*, vii, 295.

[26. ATH CLIATH LA CONNACHTA.]—Ath cliath la Connactu,
canas r[o]hainm*niged?*
Ni *ansa* .1. Cliath sciach ꝝ droigean dorigenseat na *secht*
Maine .1. *secht* meic[1] Meidbi Cruach*an* .1. Maine Aithremail ꝝ
Maine Má*thremail* ꝝ M*aine* Mingar, M*aine* Morgor, M*aine* Ann-
dae, M*aine* Mo-epert .1. mo a choimpert ꝝ a adbur, Maine *Con*-
dagaib uile, ꝝ Crochen[2] Crod*erg* inailt Edaine—is uaithe ainmni[g]ter Mag Cruach*an*. It eat sin rolasat na cliatha [13b 2]
fria hocu M*u*man ic tabairt[3] tana bo Darthada ingine Gegamain
(*sic*). Dodos-farraid cobair iardain a Cruach*ain*. Unde Ath Cliath.

> Na *secht* Maine, linaib gal,
> gniset fri feraib M*u*man
> cliatha draigin, data tra,
> for tánaid[4] bó Darthadha.

A hurdle (*cliath*) of whitethorn and brambles the seven Maines
made, to wit, the seven sons of Maine of Cruachu, even Maine
Fatherlike, and Maine Motherlike, and Maine Míngor, Maine
Mórgor, Maine Andae, Maine Mó-epert (greater his conception
and his substance), Maine Con-da-gaib uili, and Crithcen Croderg,
Etáin's handmaid—from her Mag Cruachan is named. Those
are they who set the hurdles (in the ford) against the warriors of
Munster after taking the drove of the kine of Dartaid, daugh-
ter of Regaman. Afterwards help came to them from Cruachu.
Hence Ath Clíath ("Ford of Hurdles").

> The seven Maines, with numbers of valours,
> Against the men of Munster wrought
> Hurdles of brambles, pleasant indeed.
> On the Driving of Dartaid's cows.

Also in BB. 382 a 30 ; H. 40 a ; Lec. 481 a ; and R. 110 a 2 ; where it is called
Ath Cliath oc Medraige, the "Ford of Hurdles at Medraige", now Maaree in
Ballynacourty parish, in the co. Galway.
The story relates to an incident in the tale of the *Táin Bó Dartada*, of which
there are copies in H. 2. 16, and Egerton 1782, and a fragment in *Lebar na
hUidre*, p. 20, col. 2.
Queen Maive refers to the seven Maines in the *Táin Bó Cualnge*, LL. 57 a.
They were her sons by Ailill. Their names are explained in the *Coir Anmann*,
H. 3. 18, p. 589 a. Maine Athremail and M. Máthremail are mentioned in LL. 90 b
11. Maine Andoe's death is described *ibid.*, 91 a 43.

[27. MAG CRUACHAN.]—Mag Cruach*an*, canas rohainm*niged ?*
Ni *ansa* .1. Cruach*u* no Crochen[5] inailt Etaine dodeochaidh

---

[1] MS. repeats.   [2] MS. crithcen.   [3] MS. repeats.   [4] MS. tanaig
bo.   [5] MS. croiten.

The Bodleian Dinnshenchas.

for aithedh la Midir Bri Leith a hOenuch Oeng*usa*. Robo cara
do saidi Sinech Sidi Cruach*an*. Taraill leiss ara dili dia accallaim.
F*or*fostait i suidiu. Dorumenair Etain co mba la Midir in sid sin.
"[*In* hí] do treb-su inso?" ol Etain. "Acc son," ol Midir, "is
ness[a] sair do turccabail *grén*e bail mo treibi-se," ol Midhir, "inda
inso." "*Ceist*, ciaso buaid duinne tadall in tsída¹ sa?" ol Cro-
chen.² "Bidh th' ainm bias *for*sin mag sin, co bráth³ .1. Magh
Crochan," ˥ is de sin fil Raith Maige Crochan .1. do Crochain
inailtt Etaine, fodaigh robo crod*er*g [in cenn bai fuirri] cona hab-
raib uile ac*us* a habratchur.⁴ Unde Mag Cruach*an*.

Crochen Crod*er*g, cruthmar, caem,
inailt Etaine conna[i]g,
dia luid la Midir Bri Leith
isi fo[fh]uair na deithi in raith.

Cruachu, or Crochen, handmaid of Etáin, who eloped with
Mider of Brí Léith from Oenach Oengusa. To him Sinech of Síd
Cruachan was a friend. She (Etáin) went with him because of
her fondness for him, to converse with him. They were detained
in Síd Cruachan for nine watches. So Etáin thought that that
síd (fairy-mound) belonged to Mider. "Is this thy dwelling?"
she asked. "Nay," said Mider : "eastward, nearer to sunrise
than this, is the place of my dwelling." "What profit, then,
have we in visiting this fairy-mound?" says Crochen. "That
plain will bear thy name for ever, to wit, 'Mag Cróchan'." And
hence is Raith Maige Cruachan ("the Earthwork of Cruachu's
Plain"), from Cruachu, Etáin's handmaid, (so called) because her
head was blood-red, together with her eyebrows and eyelashes.
Hence "Mag Cruachan".

Crochen Cróderg, shapely, beautiful,
Etáin's handmaid, asked.
When she went with Mider of Brí Léith
She obtained the earthwork as her *deithe* (?).

Also in LL. 170a, 43; BB. 384a 1 ; H. 42b; Lec. 484 b ; where the title is
Rath (or Ráith) *Crúachan*, now Rathcroghan, in the co. Roscommon.
Magh Cruachna, in the co. Roscommon, lies between the towns of Roscommon
and Elphin, Castlereagh and Strokestown.
As to Mider's elopement with Etáin, see LU. 130 b-132, and O'Curry, *M. and C.*,
ii, 192-194.

[28. MAG TARBGAI.]—Mag Tarbgai canas rohainmni[g]ed?
Ni *ansa* .1. do comrac ˥ do gleicc na da tarb .1. Findbennaig
˥ Duind Chuailnge ia[r] tabairt na tana im Chnoc Tarbgai.
Unde Mag Tarbgai.
Findloch .1.⁵ loch Findbennaigh, do bas ind [Fh]indbennaig
on Dund Chuailgne⁶ isind loch, *con*id[d]e asb*er*ar Findloch. Unde
poeta dixit :

¹ MS. maga.   ² MS. crothcen.   ³ MS. brath.   ⁴ MS. abrachttur.
⁵ MS. .1. Findloch.   ⁶ MS. cluailgne.

The Bodleian Dinnshenchas.

Mag Tarbga canas roraidéd ?
do gleicc na tarb tennsaiteac[h] :
t*r*ia bass in Find do mormoch
de dogarar in Findloch.

From the conflict and contest of the two bulls, Findbennach
("White-horned") and Donn Cuailnge ("the Dun of Cuailnge"),
after the drove was taken at Cnoc Tarbgai.
Findloch, the lake of Findbennach, from the death of the
Findbennach (caused) by the Donn Cuailnge in the lake.
Whence is said "Findloch", and the poet said :

> Mag Tarbga, whence was it spoken?
> From the contest of the strong-sated bulls.
> Thro' the death of the Find very early,
> Thence the Find-loch is called.

Also in LL. 166 b 47.
Mag Tarbgai is not identified.
As to the two bulls, see above, *s.v.* Luimnech.   Their deaths are described in
LL. 104 a, and in O'Curry's *Lectures*, pp. 39, 40.
Findloch.   I know not whether this lake is the same as Findloch in Cera, now
Carra, in the co. Mayo, as to which the following graceful legend is told in prose
in R. 112 b 2, H. 44 b, and Lec. 487 a ; and in verse, LL. 158 b :
, Enlaithe Thire Tairrngire dodechad*ar* do fhailti f*r*i Pat*r*aic dia mbói a Cruachoin
Aigle, co ro fersatar gleic dia n-itib frisin loch, coro[b] find[ith]ir lemhnacht, 7 is
ed adberdís : "A chobair Gaedhel, tair, tair 7 toirche!"   Ba hí sin tochuiriudh
Patraic leo, conus-toracht Patraic, 7 coros-bennach in loch.   Conid aire sin
asb*er*ar Findloch hi Ceru.
A flock of birds of the Land of Promise came to welcome S. Patrick when he
was on Cruachu Aigle, and with their wings they smote the lake so that it became
whiter than new milk.   And this they were saying : "O help of the Gael, come,
come and come hither !"   That was their invitation to Patrick.   So he came and
blessed the lake.   Wherefore it is called Findloch ("White lake") in Cera.

[29. Loch Neill.]—Loch Neill, canas rohainmn*iged*?
Ni *ansa* .1. Niall mac[1] Ennai Aignig, m*ai*c Aeng*us*a Tuirmigh,[2]
m*ai*c Ai*l*ella Caisfhiaclaich, is e ropo toisseach dibergach nEr*enn*
i flaith Conaill Cromdeirg m*ai*c Labradha Luchta.   Dodeocha*id*
for lurg mucc nDreibrinde dia lotar a Sidh Collamrach condas-
fuair i nDairi Tarbgai.   Imrachtatar na mucca[3] reimib eitir con-
aib ˥ firu iar futt Maigi Ai, fodaig rop ead[4] ainm con Ennai Aig-
nig [Feib rancatar in loch] [14ª 1] robaded Niall ann ˥ a coin ˥ a
dibergaig.   Unde Loch Neill.

> Robaidhedh Niall[5] cé*t*aib cenn
> *for* lurg do mucc, a Dreibrenn ;
> robo p*r*imhcelcgach, tor tenn,
> toseach dibergach Er*enn*.

Niall, son of Enna Aignech, son of Oengus Turmech, son of
Ailill of the Twisted Teeth ; he was the leader of the brigands
of Ireland in the reign of Conall Cromderg, son of Labraid

---

[1] MS. inserts mc.   [2] MS. tuirmidh.   [3] MS. muccca.   [4] MS. eat.
[5] MS. co.

Luchta. He went on the track of the swine of Drebrenn, when they issued from Síd Collamrach, till he found them in the oak-wood of Tarbga. The swine fled (?) before them, both hounds and men, along the Plain of Ai—for that, Ai, was the name of Enna Aignech's hound. As they reached the lough, Níall was drowned therein with his dogs and his robbers. Hence " Loch Néill".

> Niall, with hundreds of chiefs, was drowned
> On the track of thy swine, O Drebrenn!
> He was a prime traitor, a strong tower,
> The leader of the brigands of Ireland.

Also in LL. 167 a 2; BB. 387 b 42; H. 46 b; Lec. 490 b; and R. 114 a 1.
A Loch Neill in Magh Aoi is mentioned by the *Four Masters*, at A.D. 1014; but it has not apparently been identified.
Enna Aignech was (according to the *Four Masters*) over-king of Ireland, A.M. 4888-4907.
" The swine of Drebrenn", issuing from the elf-mound of Collamair, must have been magical porkers of some kind.

[30. MAG LUIRG.]—Mag Luirg, can[as] roh*ainmniged*?
Ni *ansa*. Na tri Ruadcoin Mairtene is as rogabsat lorg Conaill [Cernaig] ma*i*c Aimirgen, a Muig Luirg co Mag Slecht i mBrefne. O ronn-ortsat rucsat a cenn leo fo dess co c*r*ich Corco Laigi, condas-fil a mBrefni n*un*c.

> Marbsat na Rua[d]coin i recc
> *Con*all Cernnach na cruadhgleacc :
> lensat o Maig Luirg ille
> co m-Mag Slecht na sidgaile.

Thence the three Red-hounds of Mairténe followed the track (*lorg*) of Conall Cernach, son of Aimergen, from Mag Luirg to Mag Slecht, in Brefne. When they slew him they took his head southwards to the district of Corco Laigdi.

> The Red-hounds slew in exchange
> Conall Cernach of the hard conflicts.
> They followed (him) from Mag Luirg hither
> To Mag Slecht of the great valour.

Also in LL. 166 b 41; BB. 387 b 8; H, 46a; Lec. 490a; and R. 113 b 2.
Mag Luirg, now Moylurg, in the present barony of Boyle, co. Roscommon.
Brefne comprised the present counties of Leitrim and Cavan.
Mag Slecht, a plain lying round Ballymagauran, co. Cavan.
Mairténe, perhaps = the Mairtine of Munster, a Firbolgic tribe, the centre of whose territory was Emly, in the present co. of Tipperary. *Topogr. Poems*, p. lxix. The three Red-*hounds* (*sic* LL. 211 b 3) are = the three Red-*heads* (*Ruadchind*) of LL. 166 b 41.
Corco Laigde, the south-west part of the co. Cork.
The Bodleian text of the quatrain is much better than that of LL. On the other hand, BB., H., etc., are more explicit. It seems that when Conall Cernach was staying at Cruachu, he, at Queen Maive's instigation, murdered her husband Ailill. Then Conall fled, pursued by the warriors of Connaught. When he was slain by the three Red-heads, they took his head to Corca Laigde, in vengeance for the local dynast, Cúrói Mac Dáiri, who had been killed by Cúchulainn, Conall Cernach's comrade, and the lover of Cúrói's wife.

[31. Loch nDechet.]—Loch n[D]ecead can[as] rohainmn*iged?*
Ni *ansa* .1. Dechet rathmogaid Glaiss ma*i*c Caiss, is e tuar-
gaib Suidhe nAeda uass Eass Ru[a]id. Iarna denam a op*r*a dó la
hAedh Ruadh m*a*c Baduirnn ma*i*c Maine Milscoth*ai*g rocuindigh
loog a oip*r*i .1. torud ind essa. Dob*er*t do arna beith imressain
do feraib Olnecmacht im to*ra*d Essa Ruaidh. Is aire tuarcaibad
in tor[1] la clainn nAilealla. Robai ic[c]uingid [d]uilgine na hop*r*a
dorigni. Dobreith dó go Mag Lunga .1. co Mag Loingthi, fobith
is ann roloing *for* a biud ⁊ *for* a lind, co mba mesca medarciall-
mar do lind, do loim, do eanbruithi, do iasc. Doluid iar*u*m *for*
baili[g]ud meraigthe,[2] co riacht in loch ⁊ coram-baidedh[3] ann,
*con*id desin adb*er*ar Loch nDechet, ut fabule fer[u]nt.

> Doluid Decet *for* bai[th]chai,
> iar tomailt a loingthe lae,
> *for* buaidri, cen gairi nglecc[4]
> corom-baidea Loch nDecet.

Unde L*och* nD*echet* dicitur.

Dechet, the *rath*-builder of Glass, son of Cass, erected Suide
Aeda ("Aed's Seat") over Ess Ruaid ("Ruad's Cataract"). After
he had done his work for Aed the Red, son of Badurn, son of
Maine Milscothach, he demanded the price of his work, to wit,
the produce of the cataract.[5] Aed gave it to him, lest the men
of Connaught should have a quarrel about the produce of Ess
Ruaid. For that reason the tower was erected by the Children
of Ailill.

He, Dechet, was (still) demanding the wage for the work he
had done. There was given to him (the land) as far as Mag
Lunga, that is, as far as the Plain of Eating (*loingthe*) (so called),
because it was there that he consumed his food and his drink,
until he was drunk and merry-minded with ale, with milk, with
broth, with fish. Then he went into a frenzy of madness till he
reached the lough, and was drowned therein. Hence, as stories
tell, Lough Dechet is (so) called.

> Dechet went on a foolish path,
> After consuming his day's provisions ;
> In confusion, without delight of conflicts,
> So that Lough Dechet drowned him.

Hence "Loch nDechet" is said.

Also in LL. 167 a 14 ; BB. 388 a 45 ; H. 47 a ; Lec. 491 a ; and R. 114 a 2.
Loch nDechet, Four Masters, A.D. 1256 = *Loch Techet* (now Lough Gara,
co. Roscommon) in the *Tripartite Life*, 142.
Ess Ruaid, the salmon-leap at Ballyshannon.
"The Children of Ailill", the inhabitants of Tír Ailella, now Tirerrill, a barony
in the co. of Sligo.
Mag Lunga, perhaps the Magh Lunge near Ballaghadereen in Mayo, men-
tioned in the *Annals of the Four Masters*, A.D. 671.

---

[1] MS. tor*ad*   [2] MS. meraidche.   [3] baidegh.   [4] MS. glicc.
[5] *I.e.*, the salmon there caught, not "the ford-dues", as Prof. Atkinson
supposes.

[32. LOCH CON.]—Loch Con, canas rohainmni[g]edh?
Ni *ansa* .1. coin [Manannain] Ma*i*c Lir ⁊ conairt Modh o tait
Insi Modh, co comrancatar¹ immon muicc rocriathair² (.1. rofasaig)
a tir impu .1. Insi Modh. Mani etraintis in choin in muicc ropad
chriathar lea³ co hAlbain [.1.] ropad fassach. Roleblaing [in
mucc is]in loch risna conu. Cengsat in choin 'na⁴ degaidh.
Ro[du]s-immart doib fo*r*sind loch, ⁊ ni te*r*na cu i mbethaid uaidi
cen tescad ⁊ cen badudh. Doluid in mucc iarsin cosin n-insi fil
[forsin loch]. Unde⁵ Loch Con ⁊ Muic-inis.

Cuanairt Manannain ma*i*c Lir
ocus cuanairt Modh⁶ mormir
ros-mudaig muc dia gibis⁷
ic Loch Con, ic Muicc-inis.

The hounds of Manannan mac Lir and the hounds of Mod, from
whom Insi Mod are named, met together around the pig that
devastated the land about them, even Insi Mod. Unless the
hounds had come between them and the pig it would have been
a *criathar* as far as Albion, that is, it would have been a desert.
The pig sprang before the hounds into the lake. The dogs
rushed after it. It pressed them together on the lough, and not a
hound escaped from it alive without mangling and without
drowning. After that the pig went to the island which is on the
lough. Hence Loch Con ("Lake of the Hounds") and Muicc-
inis ("Pig-island").

The hounds of Manannan mac Lir,
And the hounds of Mod the very swift,
A pig destroyed them with its maw (?)
At Lough Con, at Muicc-inis.

Also in LL. 167 a 30; BB. 388 a 22 ; H. 46 b ; Lec. 491 b ; and R. 114 a 1.
Loch Con, now Lough Con, in the co. Mayo. As to the alleged date of its
eruption, see *Chron. Scot.*, p. 6.
Insi Mod, the Clew-Bay islands, in the co. Mayo, *Four Masters*, A.D. 1248.
Manannan mac Lir, see Cormac's *Glossary*.

[33. SINANN.]—Sinann canas rohainmni[g]ed? Ni *ansa* .1.
[14a 2] Sinann ingen [Lodain] Lucharglain a Tir Tairngiri
dodechaid do thipirait Condla fond [fh]airge .1. tipra fo'tait
cuill⁸ ⁊ immais n-eicsi ⁊ colla ai ⁊ imsa écsi uasa, ⁊ i n-oenuair
bruchtas a mess ⁊ a niblath ⁊ a nduille : a n-oenu[a]ir dofuitet
i n-oenfrois fo*r*sin tip*r*ait, co turgaib rígbroind⁹ [do bolgaib]
corcarda fuirri [co cocnait na bradain in mes sin, conad he sug na
cnó cuirthear suas ina mbolcaib corcardaib,] co mbruindet *secht*
primsrotha asin¹⁰ tip*r*ait—imso topur n-eicsi la cach n-ae—co
soann cach s*r*uth frithrosc co tici in topur.
Docoidh iar*u*m ind ingen do saighid¹¹ ind imais, fodaig ni thesta

¹ MS. co romrancatar.   ² MS. ro crithatar.   ³ MS. leo.
⁴ MS. na na.   ⁵ MS. repeats.   ⁶ MS. modh mod.   ⁷ MS. ros
mudaid muc mod dia digbis.   ⁸ MS. ciuil.   ⁹ MS. ri*n*dbroi*n*d.
¹⁰ MS. isin.   ¹¹ MS. ingin do saidhid.

ni *fuir*ti *acht* soas[1] namma. Doluidh iar*um* ind ingen lassin sruth co tici Lind Mna Fele, [꒝ traghais in topur, ꒝ rolensi co huru na habann] Tarrc[h]ain. Immasroi iar suidhi, co tarla a tarr [faen] *fuir*ti, ꒝ roblaiss bass iar tiachtain in tire centaraig.
IS de sin ata Sinann ꒝ Lind Mna Fele ꒝ Tarrchain.

> Dolluidh Sinann cuairt cachta
> dochum top*uir* tormalta,
> ro[s]tib tond cen tuillem te,
> nir' bo tuilledh comraichne.

Sinann, daughter of Lodan Lucharglan, of the Land of Promise, went to Condla's Well under the sea, a well whereat are the hazels and . . . . of knowledge, and (nine) hazels of . . . . And in the same hour their fruit and their flowers and their leaves burst forth. In the same hour they fall in a single shower on the well, and it raises on it a royal wave of purple bubbles, and the salmon chew that fruit, and it is the juice of the nuts that is put up in the purple bubbles. And seven chief streams spring out of the well, and each stream turns back till it reaches the well, which is deemed by everyone the Well of Knowledge.

Now the maiden went to seek the lore, for nothing was wanting to her save only knowledge. So she went with the stream till she came to Linn Mná Féle ("the Pool of the Modest Woman"), and the well ebbed, and she followed it to the banks of the river Tarr-chain ("Fair Belly"). After this the river overwhelmed her and turned her belly (*tarr*) supine upon her, and she tasted death after reaching the land of this side.

Hence is "Sinann" and "Linn Mná Féle" and "Tarrchain".

> Sinann went a bondmaid's round
> To a well which was exhausted (?).
> A wave smote her without a warm . . .
> It was not an addition of . . .

Also in BB. 381 a 30; H. 39 a; Lec. 479 a; and R. 109 b. Versified, LL. 156 a 6. O'Curry gives a lengthy paraphrase of this story in his *Manners and Customs*, ii, 142-144. He says that Connla's Well was "situated, so far as we can gather, in Lower Ormond". He also says that five of the "seven chief streams" were the Boyne, the Suir, the Nore, the Barrow, and the Slaney. According to a gloss in Lec., *Lind Mná Féile* is Bri Ele. See also O'Donovan's note in his translation of Cormac's *Glossary*, s.v. *Caill Crinmon*, O'Curry's note on the "salmon of knowledge", *Battle of Magh Leana*, p. 97, and the same scholar's *Fate of the Children of Tuirenn*, p. 175.

[34. DRUIM CLIAB.]—Druim Cliab is ass araile ainmni[g]ud.
Ni *ansa* .i. Druim Cliab .i. is ann dognitha cleib churaig Curnnain Cosduib, dia luidh do togail Duine Barc *for* Ainnle mac Loai Lamfotai, dia mboi bli*adain* co leith occu.

---

[1] In the MS. the words *acht soas* are misplaced between *fodaig* and *ni*.

Is annsin adbe*r*t Cornnan Cossdub m*a*c Reodoirchi iarsin
togail : Is ní ní dia tiagat fir. Am*ail* atbe*r*t :

> M*a*c Reo doirchi datta[1]
> hua Curnain cruaid cennfatta,[2]
> rogni cliabu, cian rocloss,
> hi nDruim Cliab di[a] mboi ar tuross.[3]

D*r*uim Cliab, Curnan Blackfoot's boatframes (*cléib curaig*) were
made there when he went to destroy Dún Barc on Annle, son of
Loa Longhand, and he was a year and a half at them. Then
said Curnan Blackfoot, son of Reo-doirche ("Dark-streak"),
"Somewhat is the thing to which men go." As said (the poet) :

> The son of Reo-doirche the pleasant,
> The grandson of Curnan the hard, long-headed,
> Made wicker-frames, long has it been heard,
> At Druim Cliab when he was on an expedition.

Al*s*o in LL. 165 a 20 ; BB. 392 a 30 ; H. 51 a ; and Lec. 497 b.
The number of boats (according to BB.) was 150; the destruction of Dún Barc
lasted a year and a half, and comprised Ainnle with his queens.
Druim Cliab, now Drumcliff, in the barony of Carbury and co. of Sligo. See
the *Four Masters*, A.D. 871, 1187.

[35. NEMTHENN.]—Neimethenn canas rohainmni[g]ed ?
Ni *ansa*. Neim thenn doratda ann do ceithri m*a*c*c*aib *fichet*
Fe*r*g*u*sa Leithde*i*rg la Drecuinn[4] ingin Calcmail, co nderbladar
de a n-aenu[a]ir uile. Conid desin asbe*r*ar Nem[the]ann. Unde
dicitur in Capturis[5] Hiberniae :

> Ceathrar ar *fichit*, ni gó,
> da fe*r* dég sin coba dó,
> *sé* cethrair sin, calma in cuing,
> rodosmarbtha la Drecuinn.[6]

Strong (*tenn*) poison (*neim*) was given there by Drecu, daughter
of Calcmael, to Fergus Red-side's four-and-twenty sons, so that the
whole of them died at the same hour. So that therefore it is
called Nemthenn. Hence is said in the *Conquests of Ireland:*

> Four-and-twenty persons, not false,
> Twice twelve men (is) that,
> Six tetrads, that, brave the yoke,
> Were killed by Drecu.

Also in LL. 165 a 29 ; BB. 392 b 9 ; H. 51 a ; Lec. 491 b ; and R. 115 a 1.
Nemthenn, now Nephin, a mountain in the co. Mayo.
The *Capturæ Hiberniæ* ("Gabála Hérenn") should be added to O'Curry's lis* of
lost books, *Lectures*, pp. 20, 21. It doubtless corresponded in substance with the
O'Clerys' compilation called *Leabhar Gabhála*.

---

¹ MS. diatta.   ² MS. cennfotta.   ³ MS. turuss.   ⁴ MS. drecain.
⁵ MS. caputuris.   ⁶ MS. dorodosmarbtha la dregaind.

The Bodleian Dinnshenchas.

[36. BOANN.]—Boann can[as] rohainmni[g]ed?

Ni *ansa* .i. Boann bean Nechtain m*ai*c Labrada m*ai*c Namhat dodeach*aid* lasna deogbairib [dochum in tobuir] a hurlainde in duine. Cach n-aen no tegeadh chuicce ni teigedh uadha cen athais. Badar heat a n-anmanna seo t*r*a batar ic N*echt*ain .i. Flesc ¬ Lesc ¬ Luam. M*en*btis iat [Nechtan ¬] na deogbaire t*r*a rístais dochum in topair, ni thicfad nech daenna uada cen athaiss.

Luid[1] iar*u*m ind rigan la huaill ¬ dimm*us* dochum in topair, ¬ asb*er*t nad boi occa do n*ach* diamair no do nach cumachtu mani[2] coimsedh aithis *for* a deilb, ¬ dosaig *for* tuaithfiul in topuir fot*r*i do airi[g]ud a cuma*cht*ai in topuir. Maidhid tri tonna asin topur tarrsi, coro immidh (*sic*) co ro-obann [14[b] 1] a des-sli[a]sait ¬ a dess-lam[3] ¬ a des-suil, ¬ is iarmo roteag assa sidh *for* teichedh[4] na haitisi ¬ *for* teichedh[5] in topuir iar*u*m, co riacht in muir .i. in t-uisce[6] ina diaid ¬ ros-baid i n-Inbiur Bonne. Unde Boann ¬ Inb*er* mBonn*e*.

> Dia Boann broga Breag
> brissis cach fal co find-lear,
> ba Boan[n] a hainm f*r*ia la
> mna Nechtain m*ai*c Labradha.

Bóann, wife of Nechtán, son of Labraid, son of Nama, went with the cupbearers to the well of the green of the fortress. Whoever went alone to it came not from it without disgrace. Now these were the names of the cupbearers whom Nechtán had, even Flesc and Lesc and Luam. Unless the cupbearers went to the well, no human being would come from it without disgrace.

Then, with pride and haughtiness, the queen went (alone) to the well, and said that it had no secret or power unless it could disgrace her shape. And she went round the well withershins thrice, to perceive the well's (magic) power. Out of the well three waves break over her, and suddenly her right thigh and her right hand and her right eye burst, and then she fled out of the fairy-mound, fleeing the disgrace and fleeing the well, so that she reached the sea with the water (of the well) behind her. And the Inber Bóinne ("Rivermouth of Boyne") drowned her. Hence "Bóann" and "Inber Bóinne".

> (One) day Boyne of the mark of Bregia
> Broke every fence as far as the white sea;
> 'Bóann' was the name on (that) day
> Of the wife of Nechtán, son of Labraid.

Also in BB. 361 a 49 ; H. 9 a ; and R. 97 a.
Bóann, now the river Boyne, which rises at the foot of Síd Nechtain, a hill in the barony of Carbury, co. Kildare. The story is versified in the *Book of Leinster*, 191 a. See also Rhys, *Hibbert Lectures*, pp. 123, 556.

---

[1] MS. luaid. [2] MS. mino. [3] MS. deislaim. [4] MS. teithedh.
[5] MS. teithegh. [6] MS. in‾muir.

The Bodleian Dinnshenchas.

[37. DUBTHAIR.]—Dubthair can[as] rohainmniged?

Ni *ansa* .1. id est Dubthir nGuairi *maic* in Daill insin, iarsindi dorigni fingail for a brath*air* oc Daiminis, for Dairine nDubchestach *mac* in Daill .1. a marbad[1] ar tnuth ꝸ ar tha[n]gnacht, co ro leith fidh ꝸ mothar dara ferann, conad desin asber*ar* Dubthair.

Romarb Guairi Dare ndond
cen naire, ni rim rocholl,
mac a ath*ar*, adbal bét,
issa marbad t*r*ia drochét.[2]

The Black Land (*Dub-thir*) of Guaire mac in Daill ("Son of the Blind") is that. Because Guaire committed parricide at Daiminis, on his brother, on Dairíne Dubchestach, son of the Blind, slaying him out of envy and treachery. So a wood and a dark thicket spread over Guaire's land. And thence Dubthair is so called.

Guaire killed brown Daire
Without shame, he counted it not a great destruction :
His (own) father's son, an enormous offence,
Killing him through evil envy.

Also in LL. 165 b 8, 213 b 27; BB. 392 a 34; H. 51 b; Lec. 499; and R. 115 a 1. I cannot identify this Dubthir and this *Daim-inis*, "ox-island". Prof. Atkinson says, *Book of Leinster*, Contents, p. 56, col. 1), that the former place is in Connaught; but from the story of *Tochmarc Bec-fola*, p. 176, it rather seems to be the modern Duffry, in Wexford. If so, *Daim-inis* can hardly be the Devenish of Lough Erne.

[38. DUIBLINN.]—Duiblinn, canas rohainmni[g]ead?

Ni *ansa* .1. Dub *ingen* Roduib *maic* Glais Gamna roboi i fail Endai *maic* Noiss hi Sidh F*o*rcarthan. Rocarastar sen Aide ingen Ochinni *maic* Cnucha. Ron-fitirse a mbé n-aill boi inna farrid. Doluid Aide etir fairge ꝸ in sruth [ ] co rambruinded *acht* fo thir *co* ndechsat tar Cnucha.

Rofairigestar Margen[e] gilla Ochindi sen.[3] Doleicc sed*e* uball cliss[4] boi ina laim, co torchair nert in builli fuirri ꝸ doroich[5] in tuili tairrsi. Unde Duiblind ꝸ Ath Cliath Margene, fódeig is annsin docer a urchar hisin n-ath.

Dub ingen Roduib ri[nd]glain
maic Glais Gamna glanhidhnaig,
romertain Mairgen mer mind,
ba gilla ardmin Ochinn.

Dub, daughter of Rodub, son of Glas Gamna, was near Endae, son of Noess, in Síd Forcarthan. He loved Aíde, daughter of Ochinne, son of Conucha. Dub knew that there was another woman along with him. Aíde went between the sea and the stream . . . so that . . . . over Cnucha.

---

[1] MS. mmarbad.   [2] MS. drochect.   [3] MS. ochid i*n*send.
[4] MS. cnís ncliss.   [5] MS. dorroi.

Margen, Ochinne's gillie, perceived that. He shot a feat-apple which was in his hand, and the strength of the blow fell upon her (Dub), and the flood overwhelmed her. Hence Dub-lind ("Dub's Pool") and Ath Cliath Margeni ("Margene's Hurdle-ford"), because his shot fell therein, in the ford.

> Dub, daughter of Rodub the bright-speared,
> Son of Glas Gamna of the bright weapons.
> Mairgen quelled the queen of mad-folk.
> He was Ochenn's very gentle gillie.

Also in LL. 160 a 1 ; BB. 365 a 29 ; H. 38 b ; Lec. 462 a ; and R. 99 a 1.

Dublind, "Blackpool", or Dub, is the part of the Liffey on either side of which is built Dublin, *i.e., Ath Cliath Duibhlinne,* "the Ford of Hurdles of the Black Pool". *Forcarthain,* somewhere in Leinster, LL. 153 b 32. The story is noticed in O'Curry's *Manners and Customs,* ii, 252, and translated (from Lec.) *ibid.,* 288-289. The Bodleian MS. is here corrupt and obscure. The tale is told thus in H. :—

Duiublind, canas *roainmniged?* Ni *ansa.* Dub ingen Roduib *maic* Cais *maic* Glais Gamnai, ben Endai *maic* Nois *maic* sige a Forcarthain. Ben oile do Aide, ingen Ochinn *maic* Cnuchai, co ro etaigh Dub f*r*ia ind oair rofitt*ir,* uair ba drai et ba banfile Dub. Co tudchaid la taob in maro co comair treibe Ochinne, co cachain bric*h*t mara co rabaid*ed* [Aide] is ts*r*u*th* sin co lin a fualais. Co rorathaig Margine gilla Ochinne, et imsai fria 7 foc*r*d caer clis asa tabaill 'na doc*hum* am*al* cech tathluib, co rus-t*r*ascoir dia conair, co rus-b*r*uidh 7 co t*o*rchair isin lind. Unde Dublind et Ath Liag Margin, ar is ann dob*r*t a urc*ur.*

Duibh-linn, whence was it named? Not hard (to say). Dub, daughter of Rodub, etc., was a wife of Endae, son of Nos, a dweller in[1] the fairy-mound at Forcarthain. Enna had another wife, Aide, daughter of Ochinn, son of Cnucha. And Dub, when she knew this, was jealous of her, for she, Dub, was a druid and a poetess. So she went beside the sea opposite Ochinn's house, and sang a sea-spell, so that Aide was drowned in that stream with all her family. But Margine, Ochinn's gillie, perceived that, and turned against Dub, and cast towards her out of his sling a *caer clis* like any *tathluim,* and he threw her down from her path, and broke her, and she fell into the pool. Hence Dub-linn ("Dub's Pool") and Ath Liag Margin ("the Ford of Margen's Flagstone"), for it is there that he made his cast.

Hence it appears that *uball cliss* and *caer cliss* were synonyms for some kind of sling-stone. What *tathlum* means I do not know.

[39. SLIAB MAIRGE.]—Sliab Mairige, canas rohainmni[g]edh? Ni *ansa* .i. Marg mac Giuisgcaigh m*ai*c Ladan Luac*h*ra, *r*echtaire rig na Fomoire .i. Cenntar-cluass .i. c*é*t cluass boi f*or* a f*o*roesi*n.* I n-aimsir Echach[2] Muiniste rig Lag*en* dolluid docum nErind do tobhach a cissa. Rotarclamsat Laigi*n* a ciss rechtaidhi do co Belach nDeind. Rainig do*no* immad bidh dó] ní ranic nach lind, conda-gab dene im tomailt a[3] bid. Duaid[4] da*no* in carnna commor] é tirim. Dos-fanicc ro-itai dó *con*-ecmaing tart [14b 2] bragad dó, co tarlaic a cenn f*r*i cenn in tslebe, co nderbailt de iarsin. Unde dicitur Sliab Mairgge.

> Marg mac Giusccaig cen[5] gnim ngle,
> *mac* Ladain Ruaidh rechtaire,
> rontart a braga cen buaiss
> f*or* cuairt cana Cenntarcluais.

---

[1] Literally 'a son of'.   [2] MS. eathach.   [3] MS. hi.
[4] MS. hiduaig.   [5] MS. co.

Marg, son of Giuscach, son of Ladan of Luachair, steward of
the King of the Fomorians. Centarcluas, that is a hundred ears
he had on his . . . . In the time of Eochaid Muniste, King of
Leinster, he (Marg) went to Ireland to levy his tribute. The
Leinstermen gathered his steward's tribute for him to Belach
[nE]deinn. Now there came to him plenty of food, but no
liquor, and he got into a hurry to eat his food. So he devoured
the flesh in heaps, and it was dry. A sore thirst came to him, and
dryness of throat attacked him, so he dashed his head against
the end of the mountain, and thereby he afterwards perished.
Hence Sliab Mairge, "Marg's Mountain", is called.

> Marg, son of Giuscach, without a bright deed,
> Son of Lodan the Red, a steward,
> His throat dried up without water (?)
> On his rounds (to gather) Centarcluas' tribute.

Also in LL. 160a 12; BB. 370a 16; H. 24a; Lec. 467b; and R. 102a 1.
Sliab Mairge is now Slieve Margy or Slieve Marague in the Queen's County.
Belach nEdinn is not identified.
According to another *dinnshenchas* in LL. 216b, Marg was wife of the King of
Leinster, and she died on the mountain, apparently of grief for her daughter and
son-in-law, who were killed by some monster when swimming a match in the sea
(*oc immarbáig snáma issin muir*).

[40. CRECHMAEL.]—Crechma[e]l nomen siluae, canas rohain-
mnegh[ed]?
Ni *ansa* .i. Crechmhael druth Ennai Cennse*laig* righ Laigen
dorochair [and] o[c] gab*ail* algaisse do ingin macdachta .i.
Sempait ingen Bethrai.[1] Fos-fuair in druth oc imain a ceth*ra* do
etrudh, fódaigh roboi i cuairt foigde in druth as gach tir inna
roille. Rola laim ar ind ingin dia *fo*reicniud. Imsai *f*riss ind ingin
*co n*dorad beim dia buaraigh ina cloiccind, *co* ndernai sliccrig dia
cind. Unde Crechmael.[2]

> Sampait ingen Beat*h*ra buain,
> dia[3] mboi [ic ingeilt] ic a buaib,
> nir'bo lethmael in lubair,
> romarb Crechmael caembru*g*aid.[4]

Crechmael, the buffoon of Enna Cennselach, King of Leinster,
fell there when he was making an urgent request to a grown-up
girl, to wit, Sempait, daughter of Bethra. The buffoon was on
a begging tour from one country into another, and he found her
driving her cattle (home) at twilight. He put his hand on the
girl to force her. She turned against him, fetched him a blow
with her cow-spancel on his skull, and made splinters of his head.
Hence Crechmael.

---

[1] MS. bethra ai.   [2] MS. crech. ml.   [3] MS. daia.
[4] MS. caembruaig. LL. has *comchubaid*, "harmonious".

Sampait, daughter of Bethra the lasting,
When she was a-herding with her kine—
Not half-blunt was the work—
Killed Crechmael, the fair landowner.

Also in LL. 167 b 16; BB. 393 a 44; H. 52 a; Lec. 497 a; R. 115 b 1.
Crechmael is not identified.
Endae Cennsalach is mentioned in the *Book of Armagh*, fo. 18 a 1, as having a
son (Crimthann) contemporary with S. Patrick.

[41. Lia Nothain.]—Lia Noth*ain*, canas rohainmni[g]edh?
Ni *ansa* .1. Nothan cailleach di Chonnachtaib,[1] ꝛ ni ruc a
gnuiss riam for machairi o rogeinir, ꝛ batir lana t*r*i coicait bli*adan*
di. Doluid a siur fecht n-an[n] cuici dia hacallaim. Sentuinde
a hainm, Sess Srafais[2] a fer .1. Senbachlach[3] ainm ele dó. Unde
poeta di*x*it :

Sentuinne *ocus* Senbachlach[3]
rop seiss [s]rafaiss a c*r*infess,
acht nocon adrat Mac[4] nDé
nocon fagbat[5] a p*r*imless.

A Berri da*no* lotar di[a] hindsaigidh[6] dia hidnacul for machairie
dia cetamuin. O'tcondarc sí[7] in mag mor uaidhi rofeimdes uaidi
dul arculu, ꝛ roclann liic annsin hi talmuin, ꝛ benais[8] a cenn f*r*ia
*co*nattuil i*mm*[9] ꝛ ba marb. " Bid si mo ecnairc lasa muinntir
asb*er*im foclannaim do raith mo anma." Unde Lia Nothain.

Nothan ingen Chonmair chain,
caillech cruaidh di *Co*nnactaib,
a mis cetamuin, *n*gluair *n*glic,
is i fo[f]huair in ardlice.

Nothain (was) an old woman of Connaught, and from the
time she was born her face never fell on a field, and her thrice
fifty years were complete. Her sister once went to have speech
with her. Sentuinne ("Old Woman") was her name : her husband
was Sess Srafais, and Senbachlach (" Old-Churl") was another
name for him. Hence said the poet :

Sentuinne and Senbachlach,
A *seis srofais* be their withered hair !
If they adore not God's Son
They get not their chief benefit.

From Berre, then, they went to her to bring her on a plain on
May-day. When she beheld the great plain, she was unable to
go back from it, and she planted a stone (*lia*) there in the ground,
and struck her head against it and . . . . and was dead. " It

[1] MS. diaco*n*daib.
[2] MS. .1. rafais.
[3] MS. senbathlach.
[4] MS. adrad meic.
[5] MS. fagnat.
[6] MS. hindsaigdhi.
[7] MS. sin.
[8] MS. bennais.
[9] Here a blank space.

will be my requiem .... I plant it for sake of my name."
Whence Lia Nothan ("Nothan's Stone").

Nothain, daughter of Conmar the fair,
A hard old woman of Connaught,
In the month of May, glory of battle,
She found the high stone.

Also in LL., 107 b 29; BB. 393 b 20; H. 52 a; Lec. 500 b; and R. 115 b 2.
Lia Nothe in and *Berre* are not identified.
The former of the two quatrains is cited in Cormac's *Glossary,* s.v. *Prull; and ir
LL. 161 a, upper margin, we have Seis strofaiss . 1. cained 'lamentation'. Strophaiss
in scuap b's immon corp ica thabairtdochum relggi, '*Strophaiss*, the broom that
is round the body when being taken to the graveyard.' Here *stro* is doubtless
borrowed from O.N. *strá* or A.-S. *streow.*

[42. Ess Ruaid]—Ess Ruaidh, canas rohainmni[g]ed ?
Ni *ansa* .1. Ruad ingen Mane Millscoth*aig* m*aic* Duind Dessa
doroega Aedh m*a*c Labradha Lessbricc m*aic* Roga Rodaim. Is
ass tanic, a hIllathaig Maige Moin i curach [15ª 1] Abhcain eiccis.
Luid la Gaeth m*ac* Gaisse Glaine d'Oenuch Fer Fidgac. Tuar-
gaib a seol cre[d]umai f*or*sin curuch ind ingin a hoenur[1] 7 dolluidh cosin[2] inbiur, conoss-acca Aed isin t[S]uidiu f*or*sa raba. Ni
fitir ind ingen cia tir indas-tarrla co cuala dord saimguba isind
inbiur nach cu[a]la nech aile riam and. Adb*er*t ind ingen : "Bid
he inso inb*er* bis ainiu i nErind."

Ruadh ba rigan cosin mblaid,
ingen Maine Millscothaig,
robaidhe tonn tuile tr*i*cc,
bean m*ai*c Labradha Leissbricc.

Vel [quod] est uerius .1. Aed Ruad mac Badhuirnn di Ultaib
robaided ann ic snam ind essa, conid de sin rohainmni[g]ed Ess
Ruaid.[3]

Ruad, daughter of Maine Milscothach, son of Donn Dessa,
chose Aed, son of Labraid Speckle-thigh, son of Roga Rodam.
She came out of the Illathach of Mag Móin in the boat of Abcán
the poet. She went with Gaeth, son of Gass Glan, to Oenach
Fer Fidga. The girl alone hoisted her sail of bronze on her boat,
and went to the river-mouth. And Aed, from the Seat whereon
he was, perceived her. The girl knew not on what land she had
chanced, till she heard in the river-mouth a burden of seamaids
which no one else had ever heard therein. Said the girl : " This
is the brightest inver in Erin !" [And she fell asleep and tumbled
over the bow of her vessel, and was drowned.] Hence Ess Ruaid
("Ruad's Cataract") has been so called.

Ruad was a queen with fame,
Daughter of Maine Milscothach :

---

[1] MS. a hoenur.   [2] MS. cousin.   [3] In the MS. this
sentence precedes the quatrain.

A swift wave of the flood drowned her,
The wife of the son of Labraid Lessbrecc.

Or this is truer: Aed the Red, son of Badurn of Ulster, was
drowned there while swimming the cataract.   Hence it was
named Ess Ruaid ("Ruad's Cataract").

Also in LL. 165 a 4 ; BB. 391 b 25 ; H. 50 a ; Lec. 498 b.
Ess Ruaid, the salmon-leap at Ballyshannon, co. Donegal, is now anglicised
Assaroe.

[43. CNOGBA.]—Cnogba, canas rohainmni[g]ed?
Ni *ansa* .1. Einglic ingen Elcmaire rocar Aengus mac ind Occ
⁊ nis-raichesstar.   Do teclamsat cluichi n-ann[1] etir Cleiteach ⁊
Sid in Broga.   Dothathaighdis aes an ⁊ sithchairedha Er*enn*
don cluichi sin cach aidhche samna ⁊ a cuit mesraigthe[2] leo [.1.
cno].   Dolodar atuaid t*ri* m*ai*c Deirce ma*cc* Eathamain a Sid
Findabrach cor-ruccsat ingen nElcemaire hi fuadaig timchell na
mac*c*raidi cen fiss doib.   Intan rofetatar rorethsat 'na diaid[3] co
ruicci in dind dianid ainm Cnogba.   Doronsat guba moir and,
⁊ si fess fos-railangair, a cnuassach.   Unde Cnogb[a] .1. cno-guba
.1. do guba doronsat immon cnuassach ut.   Unde est Cnog*ba.*

De ata Cnog*ba* na cuan
conid oirrdairc la cach sluag,
do guba iar mbuain[4] cno fo gle
deis ing*ine* Elcem*ai*re.

Englic, daughter of Elcmaire, loved Oengus mac ind Óc, and
she had not seen him.   They held a meeting for games there
between Cletech and Sid in Broga.   The Bright Folk and fairy-
hosts of Ireland used to visit that game every Halloween, having
a moderate share of food, to wit, a nut.   From the north went
three sons of Derc, son of Ethaman, out of Sid Findabrach,
and they eloped with Elcmaire's daughter, (going) round the
young folk without their knowledge.   When they knew it, they
ran after her as far as the hill named Cnogba.   Great lamentation they made there, and this is the feast that supported them,
their gathering.   Hence "Cnogba", that is, *cnó-guba* "nut-lamen-
tation", from the lamentation they made at yon gathering.

Hence is Cnog*ba* of the troops,
So that every host deems it famous,
From the lamentation after reaping nuts . . . .
Following Elcmaire's daughter.

Also in H. 65.
Cnogba, "corruptly *Cnodhbha*, now anglicised Knowth.   The territory so called
appears to have been comprised in the barony of Upper Slane, in East Meath.
The name is now applied to a very ancient mound in the parish of Monk-newtown."
Topogr. Poems, p. iv, No. 18.   *Cletech*, a house "situated near Stackallan Bridge,
on the south side of the Boyne," *Four Masters*, A.D. 266, note *o.*
Aes ttn, "bright folk", *i.e.*, I suppose, "light elves", *Ljós-álfar.*

---

[1] MS. nan.   [2] MS. mesraid.   [3] MS. diaig.   [4] MS. muin.

The Bodleian Dinnshenchas.

[44. MAG MURISCL.]—Mag Muiriusca, canas rohainmniged[1]?
Ni *ansa* .i. Muiriasc mór dianidh ainm Rossualt focheirdi in
muir ann fo tir ך isi a ruin ind anmanna sin no aisneidhed Colum
cilli do cach .i. t*r*i scethei dognidh, ך ba si airdi cach sce*th*i dib
.i. sce*th* im-muir ך a ethri i n-arda .i. ba[d]udh curach ך barca ך
noodh, ך ar *for* anmannu in mara isin b*liadain* sin. Sceith i
n-aer ך a err sis [ך] adcuiredh suas a sceith, ár for anmandu
foluaimnecha in aoir isin b*liadain* sin. Sceith ele do*n*o fo
tir *co m*brenadh in tir, ar *for* daine ך *for* cethre[2] isin bliad-
ain sin. Comad a n-aimsir na n.Aed nobeith in t-anmanna sin ך
Colu[i]m cille. Unde Dallan dixit : "Legais runa Rosuailt etir
scolaib scrept*r*a."

No tolo muireisc moir dorala and i n-aimsir Gairb Glunrai_ie,
cor-rolinsat glenna ך fana in tiri do*n*o in leith fri muir.

No comad hi Muiresc ingen Ugaine Mair m*aic* Echach Buad-
aig[3] dia tucadh in mag sin, *nó* comad ann roaplad Muirisc.
Unde Mag Muirisc.

.*No*

    Muiri[a]sc focheird in muir mór
    dia mb̌a hainm Rosualt rigmor :
    ba hangbaidh an gnim[4] [15ᵃ 2] cen cle
    rotharrngair Colum cille.

No

    Tola mairbeisc tuile the
    *f*ri re Gairbreisc Glunraige,
    fobruchta muir, milib clann,
    fo ceitrib tirib Erenn.[5]

    Masi Muireasc chiar crechach
    ingen dian, ua deg-Echach,[6]
    b̌a blaidh buaid cen choir cair,[7]
    fofhu[a]ir in mag co mormuir.
    Muiriasc foceird in muir m*ó*r.

A huge sea fish, whose name was Rossualt, the sea cast ashore
there, and this is the animal whose secret Colomb cille used to declare to every one, to wit, three vomitings it would make, and this
was the portent of each of them, to wit, a vomiting in the sea, with
its tail on high: (this portended) foundering of boats, and barques,
and ships, and destruction to the animals of the sea in that year : a
vomiting in the air, with its tail down, while it cast its vomit
upwards : (this portended) destruction to the flying animals of
the air in that year. Another vomiting throughout a land, so
that the land would stink : (this portended) destruction to human
beings and to cattle in that year. That animal may have existed

---

¹ MS. rohainmnieed.   ² MS. ce*t*h. re.   MS. eath *u*/ bua*d*aig.
⁴ MS. inserts .g.   ⁵ MS. erind.   ⁶ MS. uade_cath*a*/h.
⁷ LL. has ba blad búair cen choir chuir

in the time of the Aeds and of Colomb cille. Hence Dallán said : " He read Rossualt's secrets among the Scripture-schools."

Or a flood of great sea-fish took place there in the time of the Garb Glunraige, so that they filled the glens and slopes of the land on the side towards the sea.

Or maybe it was Muresc, daughter of Ugaine the Great, son of Eochaid the Victorious, to whom that plain was given. Or maybe it was there that Muresc died. Unde Mag Muirisc.

> The great sea cast up a sea-fish,
> Whose name was Rossualt royal-great ;
> Ruthless was the deed, without wrong,
> Which Colomb cille foretold.

Or :

> The inundation of dead fish, a warm flood,
> At the time of Garbresc Glúnraige
> The sea belched forth, with thousands of children,
> Throughout Erin's four lands.

Or :

> If it is she, Muiresc dark, rapacious,
> A vehement girl, grandchild of good Echaid,
> It was a land of kine, without arrangement of contract,[1]
> She got the plain as far as the great sea.

Also in LL.. 167 b 46 ; BB. 388 b 27 ; H. 47 a ; L. 493 b ; and R. 114 b 1.
See, too, *Revue Celtique*, i, 258, for some of the literature connected with the *Rossualt* = O.N. *hrossvalr*, Germ. *Wall-ross ;* A.-S. *horshwæl.*
Mag Muiresce, now Murrisk, in Connaught, see O'Donovan's *Hy Fiachrach,* p. 257, note *h.* "The Aeds", the thirteen kings named Aed, who were contemporaries of Colomb cille. " Dallán", the author of the *Amra Choluimb chille,* above cited.

[45. DRUIM SUAMAIG.]—Druim Suamaigh,[2] canas rohainmn-*niged ?*

Ni *ansa .*i. Suamach mac Samguhai senc*haid* ⁊ aite Corm*aic* Conloingis, ⁊ Caindlech da*no* a buimme Corm*aic .*i. ingen Gaim-gelta m*aic* Rodhba do cloind m*aic* Tuaigh Duib m*aic* Co*n*aill *C*ongancnis in Caindlech sin.

Dia tudchaid [Cormac] aniar o Cruach*ain* Conn*acht* do gabail rigi Ulad*h* roan a haite dia eiss tiar, fodaig rofitir dofaidsad a dalta ⁊ na bad ri Ulad eitir.[3] Dolluidh [Suamach] aniar indegaid[4] a dalta dia fhosdadh arna beith tretenid[5] *for* Corm*ac.* Intan doriacht Druim Suamaigh is and atcondairc daig na hoirgni — *nó* intan tainic Tulaig nD*er .*i. dera in Dagdae mo[i]r dodosreilic oc cainiudh a me*ic .*i. Cermat, is ann atconnairc da*i*g na hoircne —a mBruidin Da Coca, co roemid a cridi hi Suamach. Oc*us*

---

[1] I read : ba bla búair cen chóir cuir. The meaning seems to be that Muiresc acquired the plain, which was a good grazing-ground, by gift, not by contract. [2] MS. Druaim suamaidh. [3] MS. *adds* a dalta. [4] MS. indegaig. [5] MS. tretenig. In the MS. the words arna . . . Cormac come next after *Coca,* lower down.

cuala Caindlech im-Moin Caindlich a dalta do loscud.[1]   Unde
Druim Su[a]maig ꝛ Moin Caindl*ich*.

Suamach m*ac* Samgubai seis,
sencaidh Corm*aic* Conloingeiss,
ocus Caindlech, comul ngle,
ba si sin a f*ri*[th]buime.

Suamach, son of Samguba, (was) the shanachie and foster-
father of Cormac, and Caindlech was his foster-mother, was
Caindlech. A daughter of Gaimgeilt, son of Rodba of the children
of Macc Tuaig Duib ("son of a Black Axe"), son of Conall
Congancnis, was Caindlech.

When Cormac went from the west, from Cruachu of Connaught,
to seize the kingdom of Ulster, his foster-father remained behind
him in the west, because he knew that his fosterling would fall,
and that he would never be king of Ulster. (But afterwards)
Suamach went from the west after his fosterling to keep him back,
lest Cormac should suffer death by fire. When he reached
Druim Suamaig, there he beheld the blaze of the destruction—
Or, when he came to Tulach Dér "Hill of Tears", to wit, the
tears of the Great Dagda, which he shed in bewailing his son
Cermat, then he beheld the blaze of the destruction—
in Bruden da Choca. So his heart broke in Suamach. And
on Móin Caindlig, Caindlech heard that her fosterling was
burnt alive. Hence "Druim Suamaig" and "Móin Caindlig".

Suamach, son of Samguba, sat, (followed?)
The shanachie of Cormac Conlonges,
And Caindlech, bright assembly,
She was his foster-mother.

Also in LL. 166 a 46 ; BB. 409 b 31 ; H. 69 b ; Lec. 522 a ; and R. 522 a 2.
Druim Suamaig and *Móin Caindlig* are not identified.
The tale appears to be an incident in the unpublished story of the *Togail Bruden
da Choca*, as to which see O'Curry, *Lectures*, p. 260 ; *Manners and Customs*, iii,
254. *Bruden da Choca* is now Breenmore, in the barony of Kilkenny West,
co. Westmeath.

[46. Tuag Inbir.]—Tuag Inbir can[as] rohainmni[g]ed ?
Ni *ansa* .i. Tuag ingen Conaill Collamrach m*aic* Eidirsceoil
rig Temrach. Intan dognithea[2] Feis Tem*rach* la Conall Coll-
amair doreclamte fir Erind, *etir* firu ꝛ mna, cucca. Dodeocaid
Fer Fiugail m*acc* Eogabail, dalta sein Manandain m*aic* Lir.
Rotog-saidhe[3] Tuag ingen Cona[i]ll Colla*mrach* dia breith less hi
Tir Ban Suthain. Rodos-fuc iarum ina collud cen airi[g]ud t*ri*
ceird ndruidechta[4] co hInbiur nG[l]aiss m*aic* . . . .[5] Dosrad sis
inn[a] suan la taeib ind inbir co ndigsed dia comairle fri Manannan, co tanic i[n] tonn tara ess tarsi icond inbiur co ros-baidh

---

[1] MS. loscaid.   [2] MS. dognitheoa.   [3] MS. saighe.
[4] MS. ndruigecta.   [5] MS. *inserts* Rodbidh '*sic*') la taeb ind inbir.

dara eissi. No comad e Manannan fesin[1] nodos-berid, amail is follus isind rund[2]:

> Tri tonna Erenn uile
> tond Clidna, tond Rudraige,
> 'sa[n] tonn robaidh mnai Maic Lir
> ic a[n] traigh os Tuaig Inbir.

Nó

> Dolluidh Fer Fiugail fuacda,
> macc[3] Eogabail ardbruacda,
> ros-fuc Tuaig, nir'bo doaing dath,
> ingen Conaill Collamrach.

Unde Tuag Inbir.

Tuag, daughter of Conall Collamair, son of Etirscél, King of Tara [was reared, apart from men, to be wooed by the King of Erin]. When the Feast of Tara was held by Conall Collamair, the folk of Ireland, both men and women, were gathered unto it. (Thither also) went Fiugail, son of Eogabail, a fosterling of Manannan mac Lir. He chose Tuag, daughter of Conall Collamair, to take her with him (for Manannan) into the Land of Everliving Women. So by means of art magic[4] he took her in her sleep, without her perceiving it, to the inver of Glass mac . . . . He laid her down (still) sleeping by the side of the inver, so that he might go to take counsel with Manannan; but after he had gone, a wave came over her at the inver, and drowned her. Or maybe it was Manannan himself that was carrying her off, as is manifest in the stave:

> The Three Waves of the whole of Erin:
> Clidna's Wave, Rudraige's Wave,
> And the wave that drowned Mac Lir's wife
> At the strand over Tuag Inbir.

Or:

> Fer Fiugail the hurtful went,
> The son of Eogabal the high-stately:
> He carried off Tuag—it was not . . . .
> Daughter of Conall Collamair.

Also in BB. 395 b 40; H. 54 b; Lec. 503 a. Versified by Bard Maile, LL. 152 b 9-34, where *Fer Fiugail* is called *Fer Fí*, the fairy tympanist of the Battle of Mag Mucruma (*Rev. Celt.*, xiii). He came in a young woman's shape, and thus obtained access to Tuag. Tuag Inbir is said by Prof. Atkinson, LL. Contents, 37, to be the mouth of the river Bann.

The story is told much better in BB., pp. 395-396, thus:—

Tuag ingen Conaill maic Etersceoil, is and roalt, i Temraig co slogh mor d'ingenaibh rig Erenn impi dia himcomed. A slanti immorro .u. bliadan ni reilcedh fear itir do imcaisin co ngabat h' ri Herenn a himthocmharc.[5] Faidi didiu Manandan techta ina dochum[6] .i. Fear Fighail mac Eogabail dalta do Manandan 7 drui do Tuathaib de Denann i richt mna dia chraemteactaib, co mbui

---

[1] MS. ifesin. [2] MS. rind. [3] MS. meic.
[4] *Canais bricht* "he sang a spell", according to the poem in LL. 152b.
[5] MS. himthochmarc. [6] MS. dhocum.

tcora aidci and. Isin ceathramad aidci *immoro* .1. aidci luain, roc.cain in drai brict suain os an ingin, conas-focaib fair co hInb*er* nGlas, ar ba s*ed* a cet-ainm. Condas-fuirim[1] ar lar _p. 396] 'na suan *co* ndigs*ed* d'iarair culaid,[2] 7 nirb' ail do a d*us.cht*[3] *conus* b*er*ad 'na suan i Tir Ban Suthain, co tanic tonn tuile dia eis cor' baid in ingin. Doluid did*iu* Fear Fig*ail* roime dia tig, 7 nomurband Manann*en* in on[4] a mignima.

Tuag, daughter of Conall, son of Eterscél, there was she reared, in Tara, with a great host of Erin's kings'-daughters about her to protect her. After she had completed her fifth year no man at all was allowed to see her, so that the King of Ireland might have the wooing of her. Now Manannan sent unto her a messenger, (one) of his fair messengers, even Fer Figail, son of ˈthe elf-king] Eogabal (a fosterling of Manannan's and a druid of the Tuatha Dé Danann), in a woman's shape, and he was three nights there. On the fourth night, however, to wit, on the night of a Monday, the druid chanted a sleep-spell over the girl, and carried her to Inver Glas, for that was the first name of Tuag Inbir. And he laid her down asleep on the ground that he might go to look for a boat. He did not wish to awake her, so that he might take her in her sleep to the Land of Everliving Women. But a wave of the flood-tide came when he had gone, and drowned the girl. So then Fer Figail went on to his house, and Manannan killed him because of his misdeed.

[47. CLEITTECH.]—CLEITTECH, CANAS ROHAINMNIG[E]D?

Ni *ansa* .1. Cleteach [macc] Dedaid ma*icc*' Sin adbath ann sin.

Nó Cletach Ere*nn* .1. clethi-ach nErend, daig na haccoine dorigensat fir [Erenn] ann sin oc cainiud Corm*aic* [15^b 1] húi[6] Cuind rig Ere*nn*.

Nó comad cleithi tech nErind ro loisced ann *for* Corm*ac*, 7 ni fir son, *acht* is *for* Muirchertach m*a*c nErcca, 7 ba mac mathar sein do epscop Mel, et unde epscop Mel cecinit, et unde Cletech nominatur.

> Fillis in ri m*a*c nErcca
> a*m*berta dol[e]id u*a* Neill,
> sirt fuil fer*n*u in gach maig,
> brogais a chricha hi cein.
>
> ISam omun ol in bein,
> ima luaidi ilar sin,
> ar fiur loiscfidir i tein,
> i taeb Cleitig báidfis[7] fin.

Clettech, son of Dedad, son of Sen, died there.

Or *Clet-ach Erenn*, that is, the roof (*clethe*) of the groans (*ach*) of Ireland, because of the lamentation which the men of Ireland made there, bewailing Cormac, grandson of Conn, King of Erin.

Or it may be the roof (*clethe*) of the houses (*tech*) of Ireland which was burnt there on Cormac. And that is not true, but it was on Muirchertach, son of Erc, and he was an uterine brother of Bishop Mel's. Hence Bishop Mel sang [the following staves], and hence "Cletech" is so named.

---

[1] Facs. Condasfui run. [2] A curious corruption of *curaig*.
[3] da*s*cud, Lec. [4] ar son, Lec. [5] MS. inma*i*c. [6] MS. hua.
[7] MS. baigfis.

The King, son of Erc, turned,
When he was borne to the side of Húi Neill :
Blood sought girdles in every (battle)field,
He increased territories afar.

I am afraid of the woman (*Sín*),
Round whom move many storms (*sína*),
For the man who will be burnt in fire,
Whom wine will drown beside Clettech.

Also in LL. 166 b 36 ; H. 14 b ; Lec. 517 b ; and R. 122 b 1.

Clettech, near Stackallan Bridge, on the south side of the Boyne. "Forty years was Cormac, son of Art, son of Conn, in the sovranty of Ireland, when he died at Cletech, the bone of a salmon sticking in his throat on account of the enchantment (*siabrad*) which Maelgenn the druid practised upon him, after Cormac had turned against the druids because he worshipped God rather than them," *Four Masters*, A.D. 266.

The story of Muirchertach's death, A.D. 527, is told in the unpublished *Oided Muirchertaig Móir maic Erca*. "According to this story", says O'Donovan (*Four Masters*, A.D. 526, note *b*), "Muircheartach fell a victim to the revenge of a concubine named *Sín* (Sheen), for whom he had abandoned his lawful queen, but whom he afterwards consented to put away at the command of S. Cairneach. This concubine having lost her father, mother, sister, and others of her family, who were of the old tribe of Tara, by the hand of Muircheartach in the battle of Cirb or Ath Sídhe, on the Boyne, threw herself in his way and became his mistress for the purpose of wreaking her vengeance upon him with the greater facility. And the story states that she burnt the house of Cletty over the head of the monarch, who, when scorched by the flames, plunged into a puncheon of wine, in which he was suffocated. Hence it was said that he was drowned and burnt." See also Tigernach's *Annals*, A.D. 534 (Rawl. B. 488, fo. 7 b 1); *Chronicum Scotorum*, A.D. 531 ; *Annals of Ulster*, A.D. 533 ; and Petrie's *Tara Hill*, pp. 96, 97.

[48. CERNA.]—Cernna, cid dia ta ?
Ni *ansa* .1. Cerna, do*no*, [mac Ailella Ólchain rohadnacht ann].

Cerna, Cerm*na*, copbrach [cá],
Callann Mellenn, Dabilla,[1]
Crinda, Cerrind, Coroi rot,
Cuillenn cairptech, is coem-Colt,
da coicfe*r* sin, se[g]da main,
do sil Oi*l*ella Olchain.[2]

[Nó Cerniam] ba hainm don sidaidhe [leg. do thoisiuch in tsíde] fil ann, cui nomen est Cerniam. Is uad rohainmni[g]ed in dind sin a soin ille.

Cerna, then, son of Ailill Olcháin, was buried there.
                    "Cerna, Cermna," etc.
Or Cerniam was the name of the chief of the fairy-mound which is there. After him that hill has been named from that to this.

Also in LL. 168 a 39 ; H. 15 a ; Lec. 518 a ; and R. 122 b 1.

O'Donovan says, *Four Masters*, A.D. 890, note *z*, that Cearna is not identified, but that it is referred to in the Dinnshenchas as in Meath. In H., Lec., and R., the "chief burial-place of the east of Meath and of Bregia" is stated to be at Cerna.

---

[1] MS. Callan*n* dabilla callan*n* mellen*n* Coltt.   [2] In the MS. these six lines end the article.

[49. CLOENLOCH.]—Claenloc[h], cid dia ta ?
Ní *ansa* .1. Cloen mac Ingir Cluanae [leg. Clúade?] cetna
cennaige dodeochaid[1] a Alpain i nEr*inn* co nduisib flatha. Is
ann adbath icon[2] loch ucut,[3] ⁊ i n-oenbliadain tomaidm Loc[h]a
Dacaech ⁊ Locha da Dall ⁊ Loc[h]a Faefi ⁊ Loch n-Ing ⁊ Loch
nGabur ⁊ *Loch* nGaind ⁊ Loch nDuib ⁊ Loch nDremuin ⁊ Loch
nDuind ⁊ Loch Ceraim ⁊ Loch Camm, et unde Claenloch nominatur.

> Claen m*acc* Ingir Cluana ce,
> carptech c*r*ichid cennaige,
> co ndussib flath, fael ros-from,
> iss ann atbath, i Cloenloch.

Cloen, son of Ingor of Cluain, the first merchant who went
out of Scotland into Ireland with a prince's treasures. There
he died, at yonder lough. And in the same year were the out-
bursts of Loch Dacaech, etc. Whence Cloenloch is named.

> Cloen, son of Ingor of Cluain, went
> A chariot-owner, a *crichid* (?), a merchant,
> With prince's treasures, a wolf (?) proved them ;
> There he died, at Cloenloch."

Also in LL. 169 b 15 ; H. 66 b ; Lec. 518 b ; and R. 123 a 1.
Three lakes called *Claonloch* are mentioned in the *Annals of the Four Masters.*
This one is perhaps *Claonloch Sléibhe Fuaid*, A.D. 1009, which is situated near
Newtown-Hamilton, in the co. of Armagh. A Cloenloch near Gort in the
co. Galway is mentioned in *Chron. Scot.*, pp. 45, 309.

[50. LOCH DACAECH.]—Loch Dacaech, canass rohainmniged ?[4]
Ní *ansa.* Dacaech ingen Cicuil Gligargluinig, ⁊ bassi a
mat[h]air Fuata, ⁊ iss*ed* rucad [e]aturru, oen ingen dall. Atrullai
uadib assin[5] purt, co nderg[é]nai a aidhidh isind loch ucut. Unde
Loch Dacaech nominatur. Unde poeta dixit :

> Dacaech ingen Cicuil Cairn
> griggechgluin[6] g*r*an[n]a glassgairb,
> ro meirb leinai, línib ler,[7]
> noco nderg[é]nai a hoidhedh.

Dacaech, daughter of Cicol Gligarglúnech, and her mother
was Fuata, and this is what was produced between them (Cicol
and Fuata), one blind daughter. She escaped from them out of
the port, and killed herself in yonder lake. Hence " Loch
Dacaech" is (so) named. Whence said the poet :

> Dacaech, daughter of Cicol of Carn,
> . . . . horrible, green-rough,
> .   .   .   .
> Until she caused her (own) death.

---

[1] MS. dodeochaig.   [2] MS. ioco*n.*   [3] MS. *inserts* und*e.*
[4] MS. rohainmniegh.   [5] MS. issin.   [6] MS. t*r*iggeglain.   [7] MS. leir.

The Bodleian Dinnshenchas.

Also in LL. 169 b 10 ; BB. 372 a 42 ; H. 26 a ; Lec. 470 a ; and R. 103 b 1.
Loch Dacaech is said to be the ancient name of Waterford Harbour, *Four Masters*, A.M. 3506.
I cannot translate half the quatrain, and here, as elsewhere, prefer to confess ignorance rather than to guess boldly and badly, after the fashion of native scholars.

[51. SRUTHAIR MATHA.]—Sruthair Matha, cid dia da?
Ni *ansa* .1. Matha mac Roirenn m*aicc* Roga Rechtaidi ríg-muccaidh Catháir[1] Moir imm*us*n-erbaigset ⁊ muccaid Quind C*ét*-cath*aig* .1. Odba Uaincenn m*ac* Blai Ballethain m*aicc* Cath-lomna Linne. Co mbai dairi toirthech i n-iarthur Maige Macha, ⁊ ni bai riam dairi bad torthaighe. Ceped aird [d]ia mbeth in gaeth tairis, robad maidhm c*r*idie do muccaib Er*enn* a boladh, [15b 2] co-ndaste umpu ic saigidh in dairi. Taraill a bolad[2] treotu Cath*áir* Mair. Dollotar na mucca fo boladh in daire .1. mucca Lagen la muccaib Cath*áir* M*áir* co Com*ur* tr*i* n-Uisci. Roreith in muccaid fo annarb*us*, [co torchair,] cor-roimidh a tulcnaim asa cind seig. Dochoidh[3] iarum do airddibad a gaile don sruth sin, co robaidedh ann, co nderbairt araile duine do bruach in tsrotha : " Ach! in sruth dar Matha !" Unde Sruthar Matha[4] nominatur. Unde poeta dixit[5]:

> Matha m*acc* Rorend co mbaig,
> ba rigmuccaid co robaig,
> doluidh fon sruthair snamaig,
> m*acc* Rogha[6] co rodanaib.

Matha, son of Roiriu, son of Roga the Law-giver, was the royal swineherd of Cathair the Great. He and the swineherd of Conn of the Hundred Battles, namely, Odba Uanchenn, son of Blae Broad-limb, son of Cathlomna Linne, contended together. There was a fruitful oakwood in the west of the Plain of Macha, and never has there been an oakwood more fruitful. From what point soever the wind would blow over it, the odour thereof would be a heart-break to the swine of Ireland, so that they went mad in seeking the oakwood. The odour reached the herds of Cathair the Great. Following the odour of the oakwood went the swine, that is, the swine of Leinster together with the swine of Cathair the Great, as far as the Meeting of Three Waters. The swineherd ran to drive them away, and he fell, and his frontal bone broke out of his head. So he went to quench his ardour with that stream, and was drowned therein. And a certain man exclaimed from the brink of the stream, " Ah! the stream (*sruth*) over (*dar*) Matha !" Hence " Sruthar Matha".

> Matha, son of Roiriu, with battle,
> Was a royal swineherd till he contended.

---

[1] MS. rectaige rimuccaidhi catair.   [2] MS. odhba.   [3] MS. docoigh.
[4] MS. sruth armatha.   [5] MS. dicitur.   [6] MS. rodha.

The Bodleian Dinnshenchas.

He went under the buoyant stream,
Roga's son with great gifts."

Also in LL. 169 a 50; BB. 404 b 31; H. 65 a; Lec. 514 b; and R. 120 a 1.
Sruthair Matha is not identified. It must have been somewhere near "the
Meeting of the Three Waters" (Suir, Nore, and Barrow), *i.e.*, near Waterford.
Cathdir Mór, over-king of Ireland, A.D. 120-122. Conn of the Hundred Battles,
A.D. 123-157.

[52. Mag n-Itha.]—Mag n-Itha, cid dia ta?
Ni ansa .i. Mag [n-Itha] o Ith macc Breogain romarbad ann i
cath fri ssluag siabra 7 fri Tuatha De Danand.
N[ó] dial-luidh Ith macc Breogain a hEspain xxx. [long] co
hIrrus Corco-duibne i nErinn dolluid iar fud Erenn fo tuaidh[1]
[co hAilech] Neit, ait a mbatar tri ri[g] Erenn im Nectain Laim-
derg rig na Fomore .i. Macc Cuill, Macc Cecht, Macc Grene. O
robatar ag tnuth 7 ag format fri hIth ar amaindsi, co timnais
celeabradh doib co ndolluid[2] uaidib co Mag n-Itha 7 a marbad
ara febas 7 ara indracus. Conid dia digail[3] dolluid Lug macc mna
Itha .xxx. long. Unde dicitur:

IT[H] marc Breogain, buaid ní bladh,
im-Maigh Itha romarbadh[4]:
dofuccsat[5] fir i cruth cacht
ar tnuth ocus ar format.

Mag n-Itha, the Plain of Ith, from Ith, son of Breogan, who
was killed there in battle against a host of spectres and against
the Tuatha Dé Danann.

Or when Ith, son of Breogan, went out of Spain with thirty
ships to Irrus Corco-duibne, in Erin, he fared throughout Ireland
northwards to Ailech Néit, a place wherein, with Nechtain Red-
hand, King of the Fomorians, were three kings of Ireland, to
wit, Macc Cuill, Macc Cecht, and Macc Gréne. Since out of
bitterness they were spiteful and envious towards Ith, he bade
them farewell, and went on to Mag n-Itha, where he was killed,
because of his goodness and his worth. Wherefore, to avenge
him, Lugh, son of Ith's wife, sailed (to Ireland) with thirty ships.
Whence is said:

Ith, son of Breogan, a victory not fame,
In Mag n-Itha was killed.
Men in the form of slaves despatched him
For spite and for envy.

Also in BB. 399 a 48; H. 58 a; Lec. 507 a; and R. 116 a 2.
Mag nItha seems the plain along the river Finn, in the barony of Raphoe,
co. Donegal, now called the Lagan, rather than Magh Itha Fothairt, in the
co. Wexford. *Ailech Néit*, the palace of the northern Irish kings, on a hill near
Derry. *Corco Duibne*, now Corcaguiny, in Munster.
Ith, son of Breogan, one of the Spanish invaders of Ireland. Keating, p. 180.
Mac Cuill, Mac Cecht, and Mac Gréne, were the three last kings of the Tuatha
Dé Danann. See *Four Masters*, A.M. 3471, 3500.

---

[1] MS. tuaigh. [2] MS. dolluig. [5] MS. digai il.
[4] MS. romarbagh. [5] MS. *repeats* dofucsat.

INDEX OF PLACES.

WHITLEY STOKES.